REGENT'S   **Park Campus**

From HGTV and the Food Network to *Keeping Up With the Kardashians*, television is preoccupied with the pursuit and exhibition of lifestyle. *Lifestyle TV* analyzes a burgeoning array of lifestyle formats on network and cable channels, from how-to and advice programs to hybrid reality entertainment built around the cultivation of the self as project, the ethics of everyday life, the mediation of style and taste, the regulation of health and the body, and the performance of identity and "difference." Ouellette situates these formats historically, arguing that the lifestyling of television ultimately signals more than the television industry's turn to cost-cutting formats, niche markets and specialized demographics. Rather, Ouellette argues that the surge of reality programming devoted to the achievement and display of lifestyle practices and choices must also be situated within broader socio-historical changes in capitalist democracies.

Laurie Ouellette is Associate Professor of Media Studies in the Departments of Communication and Cultural Studies and Comparative Literature at the University of Minnesota. She writes about television, social theory and consumer culture, and is the co-author of *Better Living Through Reality TV: Television and Post-Welfare Citizenship* and editor of *A Companion to Reality Television*, among other books.

Routledge Television Guidebooks

The Routledge Television Guidebooks offer an introduction to and overview of key television genres and formats. Each guidebook contains an introduction, including a brief history; defining characteristics and major series; key debates surrounding themes, formats, genres, and audiences; questions for discussion; and a bibliography of further reading and watching.

LIFESTYLE TV

LAURIE OUELLETTE

Routledge
Taylor & Francis Group

NEW YORK AND LONDON

First published 2016
by Routledge
711 Third Avenue, New York, NY 10017

and by Routledge
2 Park Square, Milton Park, Abingdon, Oxon OX14 4RN

Routledge is an imprint of the Taylor & Francis Group, an informa business

Library of Congress Cataloging in Publication Data
Ouellette, Laurie.Lifestyle TV/Laurie Ouellette.
pages cm.—(Routledge television guidebooks)
Includes bibliographical references and index.
ISBN 978-1-138-78484-0 (hardback) –
ISBN 978-1-138-78485-7 (pbk.) –
ISBN 978-1-315-76813-7 (ebook)
1. Reality television programs—History and criticism.
2. Makeover television programs—History and criticism.
3. Lifestyles. I. Title.
PN1992.8.R43O86
2016791.45′6—dc
232015035953

ISBN: 978-1-138-78484-0 (hbk)
ISBN: 978-1-138-78485-7 (pbk)
ISBN: 978-1-315-76813-7 (ebk)

Typeset in Joanna MT Std
by Swales & Willis Ltd, Exeter, Devon, UK

Printed and bound in the United States of America by Publishers Graphics,
LLC on sustainably sourced paper.

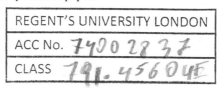

TABLE OF CONTENTS

LIST OF ILLUSTRATIONS

FIGURES

ACKNOWLEDGMENT

Thanks are in order to Erica Wetter for commissioning this book and to my students, from whom I have learned so much.

INTRODUCTION

In 2013, a teaser for a new TV program called *Meet The Tanners* went viral in the United States. In the promotion, we meet an actual family unusually devoted to sun tanning. Cast members wearing colorful swimsuits and sunglasses confess an obsessive love of the sun and converse about daily tanning regimens and "spiking vitamin D levels" while soaking up the afternoon rays in their suburban backyard. Tensions erupt when a bottle of suntan lotion goes missing and a sassy teenager faces the ultimate punishment of being "sent to the shade." Abruptly, the dramatic music subsides and the scene cuts to a black screen with the words: "The fact that you thought this was a real show says a lot about the state of TV," followed by the hashtag #TVGONEWRONG. *Meet the Tanners* was a parody, designed to poke fun at the surge of reality entertainment built around the lives—and lifestyles—of real people in recent years.

The joke was part of a branding campaign for public television affiliate WNET in New York City. The station distributed promotions for fake shows on nonexistent channels like The Culture Network (TCN) and Think, in order to position WNET as a channel for more "authentic" cultural and educational programming. Interestingly, all the spoofs singled out unscripted programming as the pressing "problem" with television today. Exemplifying the dregs of the medium were productions that fused entertainment and fact to showcase the authentic tastes, identities, occupations, leisure practices and problems of ordinary individuals and families. Teasers for shows like *Long Island Landscapers*, *Married to a Mime* and *Knitting Wars* skewered the TV industry's search for new twists on redundant themes with negligible social or cultural value. The real people who appeared on the shows were caricaturized as unintelligent, self-absorbed, phony and unworthy of media attention, and the audience for such fare was taken as indiscriminating and gullible.

The spoofs were picked up by news outlets and circulated widely on social media. This media blitz could have been an opportunity to discuss the aims and conventions of nonfiction lifestyle and reality programming, and the societal conditions in which it has proliferated and thrived. Unfortunately, these questions were eclipsed by mockery. The humor rested on an assumed hierarchy of *good* versus *bad* television, in which artistry and serious engagement with public issues are valued over ritualized entertainment and quotidian attention to private matters. According to this hierarchy, legitimated forms of television—such as the documentaries and "quality" dramas shown on public television and premium cable channels—are more complex, original, authentic and socially relevant than the run-of-the-mill entertainment that dominates TV schedules (Newman and Levine 2011). This cultural ranking system is pervasive, perpetuated by critics and scholars alike. For example, academic guides to specific TV programs and genres tend to highlight especially innovative and prestigious "exceptions to the rule" about television. Likewise, when TV viewers characterize an unscripted show like *Dance Moms* (2011–) or *Chopped* (2009–) as a "guilty pleasure," they are acknowledging its questionable value. The *Meet the Tanners* parody was hilarious, in part, because the mutating varieties of unscripted entertainment that pervade television culture are especially apt to be classified as trivial, formulaic and contrived.

Such programs deserve more thoughtful analysis. The programming trends spoofed by WNET are part of the *lifestyling of television* in recent decades,[1] a phenomenon that raises critical questions about mediated self-making and everyday life. Since the 1990s, a burgeoning slice of U.S. television has been preoccupied with questions and problems of how to be, how to act, what to do and how to live (Giddens 1991, 70). Across daytime

Figure I.1 WNET in New York commissioned a promotion for a fake reality show called *Meet the Tanners* about a family unusually devoted to sun tanning.

and primetime, major broadcast network and specialized cable channels, a large swatch of popular nonfiction and reality entertainment programming is devoted to demonstrating how to achieve idealized notions of the "good life," transforming real people into "better" selves, and documenting how celebrities, as well as ordinary people and subcultures, perform their identities and conduct their daily lives. The turn to lifestyle has unfolded across a range of how-to, advice and makeover programs, and has crept into hybrid formats that mix and match elements of instruction, documentary and popular entertainment (including game shows, sitcoms and soap operas). Pitched as pleasurable and useful, not dry or abstract, this programming presents knowledge and advice about everyday life in sensual, emotional, amusing and suspenseful packages.

Television's rising concern with self-making and lifestyle intersects with broader historical developments, including the erosion of distinctions between public and private and the aestheticization of everyday life (Featherstone 1991). It is also a lucrative business connected to changes in the TV industry, including the rise of global formats and the intensification of niche marketing and branding practices (Raphael 2009; Moran 2012). The surge of reality and lifestyle programming is also imbricated in the social and political dynamics of late modern societies. The invitation to fashion ourselves perpetuates and enables the logic of *individualization*, or the idea that social identity is less fixed, and more flexible and customizable, than before (Beck and Beck-Gernsheim 2001). The enlistment of ordinary people as amateur talent (and free labor) for television content intersects with the restructuring of work and the commodification of difference in late capitalism (Gray 2013). And television's investment in transforming wardrobes, bodies, psyches, homes and relationships intersects with the rising currency of self-help in neoliberal societies that embrace the marketplace as a model for selfhood and social relations, and with new strategies for governing citizens that emphasize individual choice, personal responsibility and self-empowerment (Ouellette and Hay 2008).

Lifestyle TV presents a critical introduction to nonfiction and reality television focused on self-making and lifestyle. The book examines the aims and conventions of major strands of unscripted programming, and situates the *lifestyling of television* within the economic, social and political conditions of the twenty-first century. To do so, the book draws from critical media studies and social theory. Within this scholarship, the term 'lifestyle' refers to the unfixing of traditional ways of life in late modern capitalist societies and the freedom—and indeed imperative—to approach the self as a reflexive and never-ending "project" (Giddens 1991). While media (including nonfiction and reality television) offer a plethora of pedagogies, templates, experts and brands to assist in the formation of selves and lifestyles, the beckoning to become the best "you" circulates in tandem with unexamined social norms and social and economic inequalities that shape and constrain the possibilities of self-making. The "ordinary celebrity" promised by television, and the incitement to "perform the real" for ratings, accentuates these possibilities and constraints, and raises important questions about whether ordinary people are empowered or exploited through nonfiction and reality programming (Corner 2002; Turner 2010).

The term lifestyle also refers to the fragmentation of the mass market (and the TV audience) into increasingly specialized consumer niches defined on the basis of demographics (age, income, gender, race, ethnicity, religion, education) as well as "psychographics" (values, attitudes, interests, beliefs, behavior). Here, lifestyle is understood as a type of cultural pluralism, a way of dividing consumers into lifestyle clusters invented for marketing purposes

(Cohen 2003). Lifestyle-themed television invites us to recognize—and reinvent—ourselves in the image of ready-made consumer "types," even as it promises to facilitate active (and ongoing) processes of self-making. The expansion of cable and satellite channels geared to niche audiences and specialized lifestyle clusters links self-making to a consumerist sense of community and belonging (Banet-Weiser 2007a). This programming sells tangible goods and services, from luxury kitchenware to bikini waxes, but it also provides a cultural platform for constructing less obvious *brands of lifestyle* based on symbolic meanings, expertise, celebrity personas and audience activities. In this sense, the lifestyling of television is connected to new ways of generating profit in postindustrial capitalist societies (Arvidsson 2006).

Lifestyle is also connected to what scholars call the "neoliberal project," a political shift involving the downscaling of State responsibility for public welfare, and the remodeling of government and citizenship in increasingly privatized and entrepreneurial terms (Rose 1996; Harvey 2005). Within this context, lifestyle has become the key domain through which societal problems are conceptualized and addressed. When individuals are called upon to become "entrepreneurs of the self" who maximize their choices, manage risks and accept responsibility for their own health, security and prosperity, lifestyle becomes a zone for dispersed forms of "governing at a distance" (Rose 1996). Both public and private agencies (including non-profit organizations, charities and corporations) play a role in shaping and guiding citizens to adopt healthy lifestyles and self-actualizing ambitions. The informally instructional and transformative impetus of so much lifestyle and reality programming makes television potentially compatible with (and useful to) the neoliberal project. *Lifestyle TV* situates the proliferation of lifestyle-themed programming as a platform for self-making, a dimension of marketing and branding strategies, and a cultural technology for shaping and regulating citizens.

THE LIFESTYLING OF TELEVISION

The *lifestyling of television* operates across a wide range of cooking, travel, fitness, fashion, etiquette, dating, shopping, home decorating, sex, health, finance, parenting, property, weight loss, makeover, property and self-help programs. This programming draws from earlier hobby and instructional genres, which have largely been subsumed into lifestyle and reality entertainment. While formal skill acquisition (such as learning to sew a button or repair a roof) has declined as lifestyle formats have become more entertaining and hybrid reality formats brought drama and spectacle to the mix (Brunsdon 2003, 2004), the programs discussed in this book are instructional in a practical, everyday sense of teaching TV viewers who to be and how to live. Featuring a proliferating array of lifestyle experts who double as TV personalities (Lewis 2008), these programs circulate idealized visions of the "good life" (Berlant 2011), as well as aspirational identities and practical resources (advice, knowledge, products, brands) for reflecting upon, stylizing and improving ourselves, our families and our daily environments. Lifestyle-themed programs celebrate and incite consumerism, but they also guide and shape the lifestyle habits and choices of individuals conceived as the "free agents" of their fates and futures.

How-to, advice-oriented and makeover programs are occasionally connected to specific ethical frameworks (such as green living) or peer-based ethical explorations of identity and selfhood among marginalized communities, such as girls and young women (*Girl Code*, 2013–), drag queens (*RuPaul's Drag Race*, 2009–) and transgender people (*I Am Cait*, 2015–). Other times, lifestyle-themed programs are also connected to broader campaigns, orchestrated by private and public "partners," to promote desired behaviors such as delayed parenting and healthy eating. The shaping and guiding of citizens can also unfold less formally when lifestyle advice intersects with the aims of public policy or the expectations placed on citizens. Since the 1990s, the values associated with the free market (risk, investment, competition, audit and self-branding) have come to bear on the idealized selves and lifestyles promoted by U.S. television. The ideal of *self-enterprise*, or the assumption that people should conceive of themselves and their everyday lives in calculated economic terms, cuts across the proliferating spheres of self-fashioning and lifestyle formation, from fashion to romance. This enterprising model of subjectivity reworks earlier discourses of meritocracy, self-invention and the American Dream, and contributes to the controversial assumption that collective activism and social movements for equality are no longer needed (Miller 2007; Weber 2009).

The slue of workplace reality shows and televised competitions involving fashion designers, home decorators, top chefs, stylists, models, celebrity hairdressers, personal trainers, professional shoppers, brand ambassadors and other "cultural intermediaries" who play a role in shaping tastes, aspirations, body and beauty ideals and consumer preferences is also indicative of the turn to lifestyle. These programs take us inside the culture and glamour industries, partly demystifying the professional mediation of identity and lifestyle, while also stitching the "aestheticization of everyday life" into everyday vocabularies and rituals (such as TV watching). Integrating elements of soap opera and suspense, programs about intermediaries allow TV viewers to become invested in human characters and outcomes of contests, and make the tastes, knowledges and skills of "top" experts in the fields of fashion, cuisine, fitness and other lifestyle fields more visible.

These shows allow some intermediaries to brand themselves as celebrity experts and establish lucrative merchandise lines (Lewis 2008); they also narrate the "realities" of work in Western postindustrial societies, where manufacturing is increasingly outsourced and profit is generated from culture, information, services and brands (Hearn 2008). Work often becomes an extension of identity formation in shows about real-life cultural intermediaries: the labor of stylizing people and products is presented as an outlet for creativity, self-expression and self-enterprise, not as source of income or a site of labor struggles. Shows about cultural intermediaries operate as informal career guides, narrating "creative" work as its own reward, and presenting the high demands and precarious conditions of lifestyle fields as a model for work in the expanding service sector more broadly. This glamorization of work intersects with the idea, perpetuated by many reality and lifestyle programs, that work on the self, the family and the home is a pleasurable and rewarding activity—an investment in the self and the "good life" rather than an anxiety-producing or exhausting burden.

The lifestyling of television examined in this book also encompasses a spate of reality entertainment built around the lives—and distinctive lifestyles—of aspirational and exoticized "others," including tabloid celebrities, upscale housewives, rich kids, rural and working-class "rednecks," polygamists, religious sects, swamp people, ethnic subcultures, trailer park residents, teen moms, lesbian couples, extreme cheapskates, hip hop moguls, hoarders, gastric bypass patients and prison wives (to name just a few examples). This format can be traced to the series *An American Family* (1973), which documented an upscale Southern California family over twelve episodes and invited TV viewers to watch as tensions flared and a marriage collapsed on camera. *An American Family* appeared on public television and was billed as educational and culturally prestigious despite its voyeurism and soap opera elements. The first season of *The Real World* (1991–), which documented the lives of seven diverse young people selected to live together in New York City, was promoted as a socially conscious, educational treatment of race relations, despite the amplification of ratings-driven storytelling techniques present in *An American Family* (Ruoff 2001; Krasewski 2009) and the strategic deployment of rapid editing, shaky camera, hip graphics, edgy music and video confessionals to package reality in an "authentic" but entertaining format for the youthful MTV audience.

As reality programming expanded during the 2000s, programs chronicling the private, everyday lives of minor celebrities and unknown "extraordinarily ordinary" real people emerged as a staple of TV schedules. The quest for interesting and unusual people to feature on these shows has accentuated their voyeuristic and sensational elements, especially when real people cast as outside the mainstream of society are involved. What often unfolds as a type of peep-show entertainment avoids the pedagogical conventions of many other lifestyle formats: no experts are on hand to advise or judge, and there is usually no movement from "before" to "after." This strand of programming epitomizes the "performance of the real" endemic to more and more reality shows, in that real people are enlisted to self-consciously portray TV versions of themselves filtered through the conventions of melodrama and comedy, and very often steeped in stereotype. The participants may achieve a new type of "ordinary celebrity" that unfolds in the tabloids and on social media (Grindstaff 2011a, 2011b). Some, such as the female cast of Bravo's *Real Housewives* franchise (2006–), may use this exposure to pen advice books, launch merchandise lines and build lifestyle brands. This type of self-enterprise is more available to the characters of docusoaps that highlight upscale and aspirational lifestyles in the vein of *Keeping Up With the Kardashians* (2007–), than it is to ordinary people cast as lower class, unsophisticated, unusual, exotic and non-normative. In some respects, the growing phenomenon of ordinary celebrity, and the synergistic media coverage that sustains it, accentuates the industrially crafted and performative dimensions of reality entertainment built around "real people." Still, these shows continue to trade on their alleged difference from fictional television, staking a claim to authenticity and public education in the sense of exposing TV viewers to the "wondrous difference" of exotic others (Griffiths 2001).

The implicit justification for peering into the private lives of actual people cast as extraordinary, exotic or different is often to learn something about them. This is the assumption spoofed by *Meet the Tanners* and other WNET promotions. The notion that reality programs like *Here Comes Honey Boo Boo* (2012–2014), which revolves around about a "redneck" working-class white family, or *Sister Wives* (2010–), about a polygamous family, are (at least) partly educational circulates alongside the assumption that television has overcome its representational biases, as exemplified by the white middle-class suburban families featured in iconic 1950s sitcoms. Reality shows perpetuate the "proliferation of difference" (Gray 2013), but they do so in ways that "post" social inequalities and reinforce dominant norms (such as the heterosexual family). To the extent that difference is often located within the minutiae of spectacular, unusual or "abnormal" lifestyles, the televised encounter with Other people can become an invitation to observe and evaluate the appearances, homes, clothes, leisure activities, eating habits, manners, social and familial relationships, values, interests and everyday behaviors of the participants and, implicitly, ourselves. In this sense, reality entertainment built around a proliferating range of "types" is connected to, and part of, the lifestyling of television analyzed by this book.

Lifestyle TV unpacks a range of popular nonfiction and reality formats, with a focus on how television engages questions about who to be and how to live. Of course, sitcoms, dramas and TV commercials are also connected to questions of lifestyle.[2] Television as a whole has long circulated fashions and norms, encouraged consumer desires, narrated the ethical dimensions of everyday life, and brought TV viewers into spaces and situations they might not otherwise encounter. However, the dramatic expansion of reality programs that enlist "real people" and audiences to the project of lifestyle is a new development. Lifestyle has crept from the background to center stage on television. Across niche and broadcast channels, everyone is called upon to participate and the stakes are high. The invitation to fashion our-selves and aestheticize and manage our everyday lives involves pleasure and agency, but it has also become an imperative that flattens the politics of difference and contributes to the idea that we can all be who we choose to be. Television perpetuates this imperative by suggesting that anyone can achieve the "good life" if they follow the guidance of experts, participate in the right brand cultures and are self-enterprising.

Lifestyle TV focuses on critical issues and debates associated with the life-styling of television. I also unpack the conventions of reality and lifestyle programming, showing how "realities" are constructed and for what pur-poses. While other media (magazines, books and websites) also engage with questions and problems of lifestyle, television's conventions of close-ness, immediacy and realism encourage an especially intimate and affective relationship with experts and "real life" subjects. Camera work, editing and sound convey familiarity, authenticity and desire, and encourage voyeur-ism and the close observation of actual settings and human subjects. Video confessionals and voiceovers guide interpretations of the events unfolding on screen, and promise to take TV viewers closer to the "truth" behind the performance of the real. Generic elements and storytelling techniques imported from centuries of popular entertainment (melodrama, comedy, gaming) structure the televisual pleasures of lifestyle, embellish its charac-ters and accentuate its stakes. The centrality of television within everyday life is also significant. Whether integrated into the flow of everyday life in the home, or used for newer rituals like binge watching, television brings reflection on the self into the habitual zones of late capitalism. Spoofs like Meet the Tanners allow us to see ourselves as savvy outsiders, but are all imbri-cated, in some way or another, in the recent explosion of lifestyle culture on television. This book directs the reflexivity of late modernity outward—to the context for the lifestyling of television and its relationship to the wider economic, social and political conditions of contemporary society.

A SHORT HISTORY OF LIFESTYLE TV

It would be impossible to construct a canon of lifestyle and reality pro-grams: there are too many (often quite similar) series to classify, and the turnover rate among programs is dizzyingly high. Because this type of television is not considered especially artistic, enduring or valuable, focusing on the merits of particular shows doesn't make sense. Moreover, this book questions the cultural legitimation of so-called good TV programs over ordinary or mundane ones. *Lifestyle TV* maps the lifestyling of television across a variety of formats and series, identifies clusters of programming, and introduces critical frameworks for analyzing the meanings and power dynamics of recent program trends. To stage for the chapters that follow, it is helpful to categorize the many different kinds of lifestyle-themed programs and formats, and identify their historical precursors. This schema should not be taken as the final word on lifestyle subgenres, but as a basic guide to programs that are increasingly hybrid in nature.

How-To and Advice Programs

Lifestyle TV has a long and multilayered history with precursors dating back to early radio. Indeed, well before the rise of broadcasting, etiquette books, conduct manuals, women's pages, magazines, advertisements and educational films circulated instruction and advice about personhood, behavior, domesticity and everyday life (Lewis 2008). Radio took up this tradition, bringing practical suggestions about cooking, shopping, childrearing, gardening, sewing, carpentry and other topics into the home. In the US, much instructional and skill-oriented radio programming was produced by public universities under the auspices of their land grant missions to serve the citizens of their States. Local businesses and manufacturers of food, soap and other domestic products also sponsored early educational, hobby and how-to radio programs as publicity tools. When television arrived in homes en masse in the 1950s, it built on this tradition (Ouellette 2002). Specially designated, noncommercial "educational" stations presented hours of unadorned how-to and advice programs on topics ranging from family budgeting to automobile repair to flower arranging (educational stations also offered "universities of the air," with professors perched in front of chalkboards teaching courses for credit or informal auditing).

Commercial television stations also developed early how-to programming, much of which focused on domestic skills and aimed at women who were assumed to be the main shoppers for and caretakers of heterosexual nuclear families. According to historians there were a large number of local cooking shows in the 1950s, many sponsored by cookware manufacturers (Cassidy 2005; Collins 2009). When the national broadcast networks developed service programming and "magazine"-type shows for housewives, practical instruction and advice on housekeeping, family, shopping, cooking, beauty and fashion were staples (Spigel 1992). Fitness instruction was also presented to housewives, with hosts demonstrating exercises step by step so that TV viewers could follow along, emulating what they saw on screen. Early makeover programs also emerged in the 1950s, promising to solve women's problems and improve their appearances, sometimes with the help of a studio audience (Cassidy 2005; Watts 2006). Indeed, many contemporary lifestyle formats date to the earliest years of television, but their conventions and aims have changed.

For one thing, contemporary lifestyle programming tends to be less focused on skill acquisition. Early cooking shows, for example, focused

Figure I.2 Julia Child of *The French Chef* was serious about cooking instruction but was also known for her quirky personality.

on the technical dimensions of preparing food. They were didactic, with the teacher usually adopting a pedantic tone, visually unadorned and slow paced (Collins 2009; Polan 2011). Today, cooking programs are more apt to emphasize the personality and lifestyle of the host, and often incorporate entertainment conventions (such as competition) to maximize audiences. The mundane details of domestic instruction are increasingly downplayed and, as with shows about home remodeling and other lifestyle pursuits, the "real time" required to accomplish a task is compressed. There are several explanations for these changes, including the rise of hybrid reality formats that incorporate entertainment and instruction in new ways, and the expansion of the imagined audience for lifestyle TV. No longer considered only or even predominantly a feminized domestic service program, cooking shows (as with many lifestyle formats) are pitched to men as well as to women, who are increasingly assumed to work outside the home.[3] While still instructional, the lessons have shifted from technical questions of how to cook a casserole or bake a cake to issues of taste, identity and the stylization of everyday life. Increasingly, cooking programs are reworked as popular entertainment involving high-stakes competitions among amateur and professional chefs, and the vicarious pleasure of consuming televised food, or what critics call "food porn" (Newman 2013). Similarly, home renovation programs, which once demonstrated construction projects in real time so that TV viewers could learn practical skills, now condense these details, emphasize aesthetic self-expression and incorporate entertainment appeals (Brunsdon 2004).

This shift has coincided with the expansion of cable channels targeting lifestyle clusters with specialized interests since the 1990s. The Food Network, Home and Garden TV (HGTV) and other lifestyle channels have reworked how-to genres as platforms for expressing and cultivating niche interests and consumer identities. This shift was anticipated by the runaway success of Julia Child's *The French Chef* (1963–1973), which aired on early educational channels and eventually became a signature program of the Public Broadcasting Service (PBS) in the early 1970s. While Child continued to emphasize the details of cooking, she was also personable and funny—a precursor of today's TV personalities (Polan 2011). By introducing a prestigious European alternative to generic American food, *The*

French Chef attracted TV viewers who were often less interested in cooking instruction than in associating themselves with good taste and an upscale lifestyle. Indeed, while PBS was created as publicly funded alternative to the three commercial networks (ABC, NBC, CBS) of the postwar period, it can also be seen as the precursor of today's specialized lifestyle channels, to the extent that it catered disproportionately to the "cultural pluralism" of white, well-educated and affluent constituencies, especially during primetime hours (Ouellette 2009). Cable lifestyle programming was also anticipated by Martha Stewart's multi-media lifestyle empire, which rose to prominence in the late 1980s. Stewart's syndicated program, *Martha Stewart Living* (1993–2005), reconceived the feminized labor of homemaking as a pleasurable and rewarding leisure activity, and connected how-to instruction to the fantasy of an upscale lifestyle (Ryan 2015a).

Until the late 1970s, the practical knowledge and skills circulated on instructional lifestyle programs were linked to the reproduction of the heterosexual postwar family en masse. The assumption of a white, middle-class and implicitly suburban two-parent family, with mother cast as homemaker and father as breadwinner, underwrote how-to programs. The proliferation of lifestyle programming made possible by specialized cable channels, however, has placed greater emphasis on individuality, self-expression and consumer difference. This is not to say that lifestyle TV is no longer gendered or invested in normative familial arrangements, including the division of labor in the home. However, lifestyle formats have become more closely associated with the expression of consumer difference, the aestheticization of everyday life and the concern with the self as project. The search for individuality and consumer difference is connected to the expansion of the college-educated middle classes and the rise of identity movements in the 1960s, the splintering of mass culture in the 1970s, and the preoccupation with wealth and status in the 1980s (Featherstone 1991; Cohen 2003). Sponsors and brands—already present in early how-to and lifestyle programs—assisted with and have benefited from the turn to stylization of self and daily life. Given cable television's intention to attract especially *upscale* lifestyle niches, it is not surprising that so much cable lifestyle programming has catered to the identities, aspirations and desires of the educated (and often white) upper middle classes.

Makeovers

In the 2000s, the forms and ambitions of lifestyle programming shifted in significant ways. While cable channels continued to guide and facilitate the self-fashioning of upscale and aspirational lifestyle clusters, the major broadcast networks offered new types of reality programming with different pedagogical rationales. Close on the heels of the international hits *Big Brother* (2000–) and *Survivor* (2000–), hybrid reality formats (often imported from Europe) began to incorporate "real" people as subjects. Presented during primetime, and geared to maximum ratings, these programs were especially adept at fusing the codes of realism with the appeals of commercial entertainment. High-profile primetime makeover programs developed within this context, many adapted from global formats. On these shows, real people were enlisted as human subjects to be transformed on camera by experts and hosts while TV viewers watched from a distance. Built on the suspenseful progression from "before" to "after," and always culminating in a dramatic reveal, the new makeover programs magnified the emotional intensity, shock value and sadomasochistic forms of shaming and humiliation featured on other types of primetime reality television. In the process, they circulated "rules" about everyday life, from what to wear to how to eat (Sender 2012).

While the makeover was not new to television, it previously was a feminized concept associated with women's daytime programming (Mosley 2000). Shows like *Extreme Makeover* (2002–2007), *Extreme Makeover Home Edition* (2003–2012), *Wife Swap* (2004–2010), *Supernanny* (2005–2012) and *The Biggest Loser* (2004–) brought the logic of self-transformation to primetime. While some offered total makeovers, the sites of potential intervention were differentiated as new twists and subformats appeared, each involving specialized experts in the body, fashion, nutrition, home décor, parenting, weight loss and other problems and domains. Cable channels quickly ran with the makeover concept as well, exemplified by Bravo's *Queer Eye for the Straight Guy* (2003–2007), which intervened in the lifestyle choices (clothing, food, wine, home décor, grooming) of heterosexual men, and the countless home, body, psyche, wardrobe and relationship makeovers that followed on other lifestyle channels. Unlike the upscale audiences and aspirational lifestyle clusters associated with cable, the real subjects of many makeovers were assumed to have underdeveloped capacities for self-fashioning, and were often coded as working or lower middle class. As a result, experts felt free to subject their psyches, appearances, leisure practices, tastes, relationships, work life and domestic environments to especially harsh scrutiny, surveillance and, sometimes, shaming.

In the makeover program, the concern with the self as project is connected to a perceived need to enlarge and shape some people's capacities to manage their jobs, images, families and lifestyle choices. This is less about the aestheticization of daily life, or the expression of consumer difference, than about empowering people to maximize their chances and take responsibility for their self-care. TV viewers are positioned to observe and judge the recipients of makeovers through the eyes of experts, and to learn from the mistakes of problematized and vulnerable "others."[4] Importantly, this strand of programming arose in the context of welfare reform policies and government downsizing initiatives in the United States (and elsewhere). In many ways, makeover formats translated the call for individual choice, personal responsibility, entrepreneurialism and self-empowerment as an alternative to State dependency circulating in the policy and political sectors, into advice, regimens and strategies for improving and managing the self and everyday life. While makeovers are no longer as prevalent on the major broadcast networks during primetime, they remain a staple on cable channels, where they continue to help people fix their problems and facilitate the transformation of "needy" subjects into self-maximizing individuals.

The impetus to take responsibility for one's health, family and financial stability thrives across syndicated and cable makeovers on topics from dating to personal finance. On some shows, experts dispense advice directly to live callers (The Suze Orman Show, 2002–2015). Other times, the iconography of law and punishment is incorporated into scenarios involving real people, such as simulating a courtroom complete with jury and judge to handle fashion "crimes." These strands of programming update programs that once circulated on the fringes of television (White 1992) such as Dr. Ruth (1984–1991), an advice show about sexual problems, and the long-running Divorce Court (1957–1969; 1985–1992; 1999–). The logic of transformation also thrives on low-budget daytime television, where experts who double as TV personalities evaluate and counsel patients, dispense advice, arbitrate personal conflicts, mediate lifestyle choices and stage makeovers on a daily basis. Like splashier primetime makeovers, daytime's investment in self-transformation often synchronizes with the neoliberal project of privatizing and personalizing public welfare (Ouellette and Hay 2008).

Talk Shows

Daytime talk shows, which filled the airwaves with ordinary people in the 1980s and 1990s, are another precursor to contemporary lifestyle and reality formats. Each day, a host invited "real people" to discuss the experiences and problems of everyday life, disputes with friends and relatives, and (on occasion) social issues ranging from eating disorders to abortion. While experts were on hand to dispense advice, and celebrities were sometimes featured, the shows emphasized the interaction between the host, participants and the studio audience, which sometimes became lively (Shattuc 1997). In their heyday there were dozens of daytime talk shows on television, ranging in tone from the female, self-help oriented *Oprah Winfrey Show* (1986–2011) to the outrageously sensational *Jerry Springer Show* (1991–), which had the host entering the stage by sliding down a stripper pole, and employed on-screen security guards to oversee the emotional breakdowns, yelling matches and occasionally violent outbursts that ensued during the episodes (Grindstaff 2002). Such behavior was encouraged by producers, who believed that sensationalized "money shots" of people losing control of their emotions, crying and fighting, would bolster ratings. Today's reality producers deploy similar strategies to maximize the entertainment value of unscripted entertainment, including makeovers (Grindstaff 2011a).

Talk shows were socially diverse; they made working-class people without college degrees and professional jobs more visible and offered (then rare) opportunities for LGBTQ people to appear on television. While some critics deemed the shows trashy, and accused them of "airing dirty laundry" due to the intimate nature of the conversations and the marginalized status of the people who appeared on them, some scholars emphasized their capacity to democratize the nature of public debate and raise consciousness about important topics and issues (Gamson 1999). In retrospect, it seems clear that talk shows opened up opportunities for a wide range of ordinary people to share their personal stories on television—in terms that encouraged them to play to the social stereotypes and the sensationalized conventions demanded by the TV industry. The decline of the talk shows, and the rise of more authoritative, expert-driven formats that focus on guiding and transforming real people (*Judge Judy*, 1996– ; *Judge Joe Brown*, 1997–2013; *Dr. Phil*, 2002– ; *Dr. Oz*, 2009–), has occurred in tandem with the intensification of the neoliberal project.

Docusoaps

Talk shows exemplified the explosion of "first person media" in the 1990s. This term refers to formats based around the subjective experience of ordinary people, including amateur video programs, video diaries and personal documentary. The rising visibility of ordinary people on television has evolved in part from this earlier phenomenon. We can see the influence of first person media in reality entertainment formats that enlist ordinary people to perform the "ordinariness of their own extraordinary subjectivity" (Dovey 2000, 4). Video confessionals, where cast members address the camera directly and share their thoughts and feelings about the events shown on screen, are reminiscent of video diaries shot with camcorders. In the 1990s, the British Broadcasting Corporation (BBC) commissioned short self-recordings about everyday life, and circulated them on national television without expert commentary. The video diarists recorded their thoughts and feelings about topics ranging from poverty to identity, in personal and often emotional terms. The point of the project was to encourage TV viewers to learn about and empathize with the social experiences of the diversity of people in the United Kingdom. In docusoaps, breakaway video confessionals also encourage an emotional connection to the experiences of ordinary people who are called upon to "speak for themselves" to the camera. However, this is now done for the purpose of commercial entertainment, and speaking subjects are expected to accommodate established formulas, casting priorities and scripts.

While docusoaps are packaged as entertainment, they are also part of the lifestyling of television. In the process of narrating "real" situations, conflicts and feelings, docusoaps invite TV viewers to peer into the private lives and lifestyles of real people. At one end of the format are shows focusing on unusually wealthy people and celebrities. These programs take us inside spectacular homes, high-end shops, luxurious resorts and trendy restaurants, and display the ordinary accouterments of an upscale lifestyle. In this sense, they take their cue from earlier shows like *Lifestyles of the Rich and Famous* (1984–1995), which adapted journalistic conventions to report on the residences, social gatherings and luxurious lifestyles of the spectacularly well-to-do. Reality entertainment makes the rich and famous into relatable characters, fusing the conventions of soap opera, sitcom and fly-on-the-wall documentary to create emotionally "authentic" stories about everyday life.

However, these shows also lavish enormous attention on the affluent surroundings and lifestyles of their participants. By bringing TV viewers inside the private world of high-end taste and luxurious consumption, *Keeping Up With the Kardashians* (2007–), *Rich Kids of Beverly Hills* (2014–) and *Love and Hip Hop* (2010–) operate in dialogue with other lifestyle formats.

There has been a growing tendency to take curious TV viewers inside the intimate lives of people coded as lower and working class as well. While class as the basis of economic inequality is not acknowledged or addressed, a cluster of programming now takes TV viewers inside the homes and lifestyles of individuals and families cast as culturally "different" from an imagined middle-class audience (*Swamp People*, 2010– ; *Here Comes Honey Boo Boo*, 2012–2014; *Trailer Park: Welcome to Myrtle Manor*, 2013–). Lowbrow tastes, unrefined bodies, modest surroundings, hedonistic values and other stereotypical symbolic markers of class marginality are emphasized through conventions of casting, camera, setting, editing, graphics, props and voiceover. The emphasis on class difference has been accompanied by (and often intersects with) the soaring visibility of real people cast as unusual and non-normative, from ethnic subcultures (*Jersey Shore*, 2009–2012), to people of small stature (*The Little Couple*, 2009–) to polygamous families (*Sister Wives*, 2012–). Such programs cast "other" people as spectacular, unusual and exotic, even as they are also presented as "just like us" in some respects. While this cluster of programming expands the social diversity found on television, it does so in ways that often reinforce boundaries between "us" and "them." Because difference is coded in the details of lifestyle, this strand of programming

Figure I.3 Working-class lifestyle is presented as fodder for laughs on *Here Comes Honey Boo Boo*.

encourages close observation and evaluation of people who are assumed to be "different" because of lifestyle choices, not power relations. While the impetus to judge from a distance can be tempered by the construction of relatable characters and everyday storylines, the pervasive logic of the makeover has encouraged us to understand self-fashioning as the basis of personal failure and success, no matter the circumstances. The question remains whether the rising visibility of ordinary people in general, and underrepresented and marginalized communities in particular, constitutes a step toward representational democracy, or a type of economic and cultural exploitation.

AIMS AND CHAPTERS

This book introduces critical frameworks for making sense of the lifestyling of television. I examine a range of formats that document, guide and facilitate self-making and lifestyle practices, including cooking and decorating programs, self-help programs, dating shows, talent competitions, docusoaps and reality sitcoms. While their concerns and conventions vary, all of these formats contribute to the project of lifestyle and "operate" as nonfiction. Following Frances Bonner (2003), I use the verb "operate" because lifestyle and reality formats make "claims to the real" in different ways.

How-to programs recorded live before a studio audience, for example, will convey immediacy and actuality differently from a more polished docusoap aired months after the events on screen have transpired, and may make a "truth claim" (these ingredients combined will produce this particular cake) that reality entertainment programs do not. While the programs examined in this book all assert a "reasonably direct relationship with 'real' life," many are partly or even fully scripted (2003, 3). The "realities" presented are mediated by other production decisions as well, such as casting, editing, camerawork, storytelling, lighting, wardrobe and props, even when scripts are not used, no matter how spontaneous the people and events on screen may appear. To various degrees, codes of realism (drawn from the documentary tradition) are combined with the narrative conventions and slick packaging of television entertainment. While TV viewers may be perfectly aware of the stage-managed aspects of reality entertainment, the characters, situations and emotions may simultaneously be understood as relatable and "authentic" (Bignell 2014). In the end, I am less concerned with the accuracy (or not) of representation than with television's *productive* role in the social construction of reality. The lifestyling of television is important because it puts into circulation resources for assembling selves, living everyday life and organizing the social world.

I regularly watch and (sometimes) enjoy the lifestyle and reality programs analyzed in this book. As a critic, I am not "outside" the culture I am analyzing, but immersed in it. As I often tell my students, it is possible—and often helpful—to be critics and fans at the same time. I do not believe that TV viewers are "duped" by the lifestyling of television, but I do think that our realities—and sense of ourselves—are produced within particular economic, social, political and cultural contexts. The programs examined in this book seek a particularly powerful role in this process, which is why it is so important to unpack the assumptions, directives and agendas they circulate. Lifestyle-themed programming, perhaps more than any other type of television, provides an entry point for thinking about the power dynamics of the "real world." The programming analyzed here does not reflect this world, as much as it actively contributes to the making (and remaking) of selves, the commodification of difference, the creation of economic value and the self-government of individuals.

The lifestyling of television is a global phenomenon facilitated by the international trade of pre-established formats. Many of the programs examined in this book are based on formulas that circulate—tweaked for local tastes and customs—all over the world (Moran 2012, 2014). This book focuses primarily on U.S. television, the context with which I am most familiar, but draws inspiration from scholars working on reality television in a range of global contexts and presents critical modes of analysis with transnational relevance. Each chapter develops a different conceptual lens for making sense of the lifestyling of television. I have pried apart a web of discourses and power dynamics that frequently intersect and sometimes contradict for analytic purposes. While each chapter adds a layer to an introductory analysis of lifestyle television, these layers do not add up to a seamless whole. Rather, different critical perspectives reveal a multiplicity of power dynamics that coalesce in complex and sometimes unexpected ways around a singular cultural object—lifestyle television.

Chapter 1, "Branding Lifestyle," connects the lifestyling of television in recent decades to developments in niche marketing, and develops the concept of brand culture to analyze the differentiation of lifestyle networks, and the branding of lifestyles and products and people across nonfiction and reality formats. Chapter 2, "The Self as Project," analyzes the forms of self-fashioning illustrated and enabled by lifestyle and reality television, and situates the impetus to reflect upon, aestheticize and transform the self within the promises and pressures of late modern capitalist societies. Chapter 3, "Governing Citizens," introduces lifestyle and reality television as a technology of citizenship that steers self-managing individuals toward the desired outcomes of experts and authorities, and points to some contradictions in this process. Chapter 4, "The Labor of Lifestyle," situates the labor narrated on and encouraged by reality and lifestyle formats within the conditions of work in the twenty-first century, including the gendered "second shift" of domestic labor performed in the home, the turn to precarious and freelance labor, and the celebration of creative work. Chapter 5, "Performing Difference," situates the increased visibility of marginalized and underrepresented groups on reality television within debates about the influx of ordinary people in the media, the role of performance in identity and reality TV production, and the circulation of race, class and other social differences as commodities, lifestyles and brands.

NOTES

1 The term "lifestyling of television" is inspired by Charlotte Brunsdon's 2003 analysis of the transformation of British primetime terrestrial television. Brunsdon noted that quasi-instructional lifestyle programs that had previously been relegated to daytime or weekend hours were commanding more visibility during the peak "8–9 slot." This has become a global trend, as lifestyle instruction has been subsumed into hybrid reality formats, and cable and satellite channels specializing in how-to lifestyle programming have expanded.

2 Mimi White notes this parallel in the syllabus for her undergraduate course on Lifestyle Television in the Department of Radio/TV/Film at Northwestern University. I wish to thank Mimi for generously sharing her syllabus, which helped refine the focus of this book.

3 As we will see in Chapter 4, cooking programs aimed explicitly at women are more apt to retain an instructional tone and emphasize the preparation of family meals.

4 Importantly, TV viewers may not cooperate with these conventions. In their study of makeover audiences in Britain, Beverly Skeggs and Helen Wood (2012) found that viewers used a range of criteria for identifying with and judging the actions of the real people on screen that correlated with their social experience.

1

BRANDING LIFESTYLE

In 2014, eight hopeful young women competed to become the inaugural Global Brand Ambassador for celebrity fashion designer Diane von Furstenburg, creator of the iconic wrap dress, while TV cameras rolled. *House of DVF* (2014–) chronicled their immersion into the business operations of DVF, a global luxury lifestyle brand that sells clothing as well as shoes, handbags, leather goods, jewelry, scarves, luggage and home furnishings. In the debut episode, von Furstenberg describes the DVF brand as representing confidence, attitude and the "empowerment of women," while the camera pans a cornucopia of merchandise on display at the company's opulent New York City headquarters. A shot of one of DVF's retail stores lingers on a picture window displaying the designer's name, and segues into scenes of von Furstenburg being photographed at fashion shows and hobnobbing with Hollywood celebrities. On the audio track, a narrator boasts that *Forbes* magazine named von Furstenberg "the most powerful name in fashion . . . with 106 stores in 56 countries." By the time the female contenders (who have been promised the chance to "travel the world living the jet set life," while representing the DVF brand at "cultural happenings, store openings, and premiere fashion events") arrive on the scene, the series has been established as a weekly showcase for an upscale designer lifestyle in which branding, identity and consumption are closely intertwined.

House of DVF stitches a lifestyle brand into the heart of the reality competition, a hybrid genre that combines the conventions of the documentary, the game show and the soap opera. Under von Furstenberg's direction, the contestants compete to master a "crash course" in styling, public relations, merchandising and event planning in storylines that promote the DVF brand in an "authentic" fashion industry setting. What is being sold is not a dress or a pair of shoes, but rather the aspirational identity and lifestyle that DVF claims to represent. The contestants competing to play a role in this process are closely monitored and evaluated on the basis of their appearance, personality, social skills and compatibility with the DVF image. This scrutiny presents the narrative context for arguments, teary meltdowns and other melodramatic elements, and sets the stage for a subtle type of self-branding. To win the game, the women must present a commercially viable persona to von Furstenberg and her team, while also providing talent for a reality show that expects them to perform for high ratings. The women are encouraged to perform marketable images of themselves for the judges and the TV industry, in the hope of winning the prize or paving the way for future payoffs—perhaps even a lifestyle brand of their own.

House of DVF contributes to the intensified branding of contemporary life, from the television channels we watch to our lifestyles and even ourselves. The program neatly illustrates the different layers of branding at work in the *lifestyling of television*, defined as the focus on "who to be and how to live" across a growing number of popular nonfiction and reality programs. Beyond the "natural" publicity afforded by the reality format, *House of DVF* benefits from a synergistic partnership with the E! media brand. The E! cable network (owned by NBCUniversal) is branded as a programming service for "upscale, professional" fans of celebrities, fashion and pop culture, and the hub of a mediated community for TV viewers, advertisers and E! personalities, including the cast of *Keeping Up With the Kardashians* (2007–). *House of DVF's* appearance on E! situates DVF within the tastes and sensibilities of the E! brand community, and digital media platforms enhance the partnership. E! online circulates clips and bonus scenes, Instagram photos of von Furstenberg and "news" coverage of the designer's jetsetter lifestyle, and DFV operates its own *House of DVF* website, where TV viewers can find inside scoops on the E! program, "shop the episodes" for the DVF goods featured in them and browse the company's online catalog. Both E! and DVF also use social media (Twitter, Tumblr, Facebook) to connect with *House of DVF* viewers while promoting their respective brands. Branding shapes the storyline of *House of DVF*, and structures the institutional and cultural contexts in which the program circulates.

This chapter introduces the concept of *brand culture* as a lens for analyzing the lifestyling of television. Branding originally referred to the process of marking livestock with symbols to indicate their owners. Similarly, early manufacturers used visual trademarks to differentiate more or less identical mass-produced consumer goods, like soap and oatmeal. Today, branding involves more than stamping a "logo to the surface of a product" (Johnson 2013, 17): successful brands animate cultural meanings and social practices that supplant the utilitarian function of consumer goods and services and constitute active relationships between individuals and the commercial world. Contemporary branding is less about imposing meanings and tastes on to passive consumers than creating a context or "ambience, comprised of sensibilities and values" from which their actions are poised to unfold in particular ways that generate value and profit for brands (Hearn 2008, 197). While branding is imbricated in hyper-commercialism, "logo mania" and the increased commodification of modern life, it is as much a cultural phenomenon as an economic one, argues Sarah Banet-Weiser (2012). Such is the case with lifestyle-themed television, where branding provides the scaffolding for profitmaking as well as consumer belonging, advice and aspirational models of personhood and daily living.

Banet-Weiser uses the term 'brand culture' to characterize the impact of branding on our shared meaning systems, cultural institutions, understandings of ourselves and everyday practices. Branding is about monetizing our social experiences, practices of self-making and our sense of identity and belonging in the social world. The logic of branding has become more pervasive in recent decades, extending beyond the "persuasive powers" of any particular campaign to the broader "relationships between consumers and the commercial world, and the way in which these types of relationships have increasingly become cultural contexts for everyday living, individual identity and affective relationships," Banet-Weiser contends (quoted in Jenkins 2013). In what follows, I connect the lifestyling of television in

Figure 1.1 House of DVF operates as an extended branding campaign for fashion designer Diane von Furstenberg.

recent decades to brand culture, and discuss the branding of TV networks, lifestyles, products and people across nonfiction and reality formats.

BRANDS OF TELEVISION

The first layer of branding in the lifestyling of television involves what Amanda Lotz calls *brands of television* (2006). Before the arrival of hundreds of cable and satellite channels, "on demand" viewing options and new media technologies, television (like radio before it) was a mass medium. In the US, four major broadcast networks (ABC, CBS, NBC and PBS) and a smattering of independent channels dominated the medium's cultural output well into the 1970s. Programs were geared to the largest audience possible during their timeslot, and (until the invention of the VCR in the 1980s) were necessarily watched in real time. With the exception of the Public Broadcasting Service (PBS), which was created as a high cultural and studious alternative to commercial entertainment (Ouellette 2002), broadcast TV networks did not have clear brand identities. As the number of channels expanded, beginning in the 1980s, and the logic of narrowcasting, or gearing programming to specialized audiences conceived as lifestyle clusters, became more prevalent, "cable networks—and increasingly broadcast networks as well—established brands to attract certain audiences to their programming," which in turn allowed "advertisers to inundate these audiences with appeals for goods and services" (Lotz 2006, 38).

Today, television networks establish recognizable brand identities through scheduling practices, promotional campaigns, genre and casting priorities, and repetitive visual and sonic cues, argues Victoria Johnson. Together, these practices "create a symbolic field that signals a coherent destination for a viewer who is addressed and welcomed as belonging to that network's community" (Johnson 2013, 263). In the current era of more than 300 cable and satellite networks, "strong brand recognition" is crucial to commercial success in a highly cluttered cultural environment. In addition to offering a differentiated product, networks must establish a strong "connection to the viewer" that increasingly extends beyond programming into digital platforms and activities like gaming, tweeting, posting and sharing (Curtin and Shattuc 2009, 120). As television has converged with new media technologies, the promise of interactivity has become more integral to the cultural construction of brands of television as "meeting places" between consumers and producers (Johnson 2012, 17), or what Celia Lury calls interfaces (2004). Characterizing the impact of these changes, Michael Curtin and Jane Shattuc contend: "No longer do we have TV audiences— now, we have brand communities" (2009, 20).

Television's shift from mass medium to a multichannel and increasingly interactive cultural environment can be traced to deregulatory telecommunication policies and the commercial development of cable, satellite and digital media technologies. The fragmentation of the mass market, which began even earlier, paved the way for the TV industry to target particular lifestyle clusters and construct brand communities around them. Cultural historian Lizbeth Cohen (2003) traces this fragmentation to the impetus to make the Fordist capitalist system of production and consumption more efficient. As the postwar consumer economy expanded, marketers developed ways to pitch more specialized products to particular consumer niches. The move toward niche marketing gained momentum in the 1970s with the implementation of new forms of marketing research that combined precise demographic data on age, gender, race, education and other variables with "psychographic" information about values, lifestyles, interests and consumer behaviors. From this research, marketers identified "clusters of consumers with distinctive ways of life and then set out to sell them idealized lifestyles constructed around commodities," says Cohen (2003, 229). These lifestyle clusters were merely statistical profiles assembled by marketers for their own commercial purposes. However, niche marketing tapped in to a growing discontent about mass culture, especially among the educated elite, and offered new opportunities for individuals to "express their separate identities through their choices as consumers" (2003, 309).

Class hierarchies were depoliticized as marketers presented unequal access to education and income as lifestyle choices. "What consumers bought—a Cadillac over a Chevrolet, a ranch house instead of a Cape Cod, The New Yorker over True Story magazine became indicators of their class identity" and chosen membership in a class community, Cohen observes (2003, 310). As the social movements and youth countercultures of the 1960s and 1970s gained currency, and pursued identity formation apart from mainstream culture, independent and working women, racial minorities, disaffected youth, hippie subcultures and gays and lesbians were also recognized and targeted as consumer clusters. Collective practices and political struggles for recognition were recast in the vocabulary of lifestyle and consumer choice. The breakup of the major networks' hold on television has paralleled the fragmentation of consumer culture writ large. While some television programming was always geared to "segments within the mass audience" (such as housewives and children), it was difficult to target viewers conceived as specialized lifestyle clusters with a mass medium. The expansion of cable channels in the 1980s enabled the "carving up of television programming into market niches" and eventually made segmentation the norm in television, says Cohen (2003, 304). Indeed, cable's business model hinged on the ability to target niche consumer markets through specialized content.

Joseph Turow identifies MTV and Nickelodeon as the first U.S. cable channels to establish recognizable brand identities (1997). Targeting relatively upscale teenagers and children whose families could afford cable subscriptions, these networks (owned by media giant Viacom) operated not only as program suppliers, but as "lifestyle parades" that offered their target audiences a "sense of belonging" that wasn't limited to television, but also included tie-in magazines, books, videos and other media packaged and sold by Viacom (1997, 5). Cultivating a "must-see, must-read, must-share mentality," cable channels made their niche audiences feel like "part of a family, attached to the program hosts, other viewers and sponsors," which made it easier for advertisers to pitch "specific messages about how certain products tie into their lifestyles," Turow observed of early cable branding. When viewers "feel that a TV channel resonates with their personal beliefs, and helps them chart their position in the larger world," they become more valuable to advertisers as especially targetable and loyal consumers (Turow 1997, 4). This is still the case. However, brands do not simply reflect and target pre-existing social identities and lifestyles—they create them (Davila 2001). From the classification of niche markets to the programming and sense of community developed around these conceptions, brands of television play an active role in constituting and mobilizing the consumer clusters they target and sell to advertisers.

Following the success of MTV and Nickelodeon, narrowcasting has become standard in U.S. cable television. Psychographic market research, known as "Values, Attitudes and Lifestyles" (VALS) to the industry, is widely used to pinpoint niche audiences and match differentiated brands of television with advertisers and products. From Animal Planet ("animal lovers and pet owners") to Esquire TV ("intelligent and stylish men") to Oxygen ("socially savvy female millennials"), U.S. television is awash with distinct cable brands targeting specialized interests, values and demographics. While owned by a small number of global media conglomerates, the proliferation of different brands of television, each catering to specialized and "unique" audiences, has created an impression of social and cultural diversification. However, the assumption that U.S. television now offers "something for everyone" has been debunked by critical scholars who note that affluent consumers are more likely to be constituted as "desirable," and niche marketing flattens and conceals the intersectionality of race, ethnicity, class, gender and sexual orientation. For example, Lifetime and BET, which pioneered the targeting of women and African Americans as niche TV viewers, have been criticized for overemphasizing the interests, aspirations and experiences of economically privileged consumers, and for circulating narrow and often stereotypical understandings of femininity and blackness that synchronize with commercial agendas (Byars and Meehan 1994–95;

Smith-Shomade 2007). Newer cable brands explicitly targeting Latino and LGBT audiences, such as NuvoTV and Logo, evoke similar concerns.

LIFESTYLE BRANDS

The branding of television has facilitated a proliferation of *lifestyle brands* that are built around but extend beyond specialized cable channels. Since the early 1990s, a growing number of cable networks have cued opportunities for self-actualization, lifestyle formation and consumer belonging to particular aspects of daily life, such as travel, fashion, home decorating, house hunting, gardening and cooking. For example, the Scripps Interactive portfolio of "popular lifestyle brands," which encompasses the DIY Network, Cooking Channel and Travel Channel, as well as the (now defunct) Fine Living Network, Food Network and Home and Garden Television (HGTV), aims to connect TV viewers to "relevant ideas, information and solutions every day, everywhere." Focusing on informational and unscripted lifestyle programming, these channels operate as cultural *interfaces* (Lury 2004) to expansive multimedia lifestyle brands that include magazines, books, websites and interactive social media platforms (such as Twitter and Facebook).

Lifestyle brands connect the fragmentation of the television audience into specialized lifestyle clusters to suggestions for everyday living structured through commercial relationships. Sam Binkley defines lifestyle branding as an especially nuanced form of marketing that brings the "dream world of commodity seduction" into actual practices of everyday life, exemplified by the Nike lifestyle brand's famous slogan, "Just Do It." Lifestyle brands, he argues, imbue consumption choices "with explicit invocations of a good life," related in a discourse that goes beyond the aspirational imagery of advertising to the ongoing dissemination of "guidance, knowledge, and advice related by the alleged properties of the brand" (2007a, 123). Cable networks pitched to specialized interests and consumer niches are particularly compatible with a form of lifestyle branding that places television at the center of regimens and consumer resources for living flow across media platforms.

Lifestyle brands invite consumers to participate in frameworks for living that align their identities, behaviors, tastes and choices related to food, the body, the home, clothing and other everyday zones and activities with a commercial enterprise. Lifestyle brands do not manipulate passive consumers as much as they "activate" them to fashion their identities and everyday lives, and connect with likeminded individuals, within a cultural framework organized by the brand. This involves more than the circulation of commercial images and ideologies. As Adam Arvidsson argues, brands create monetized "frames of action" that depend on the cooperation and agency of consumers (Arvidsson 2006, 8). Lifestyle brands built around U.S. television channels create "frames of action" that align with the imagined interests, sensibilities and tastes of targeted consumer clusters, and establish the brand as an access point to resources (expertise, skills, products) to assist in self-making and everyday practices such as shopping, cooking, entertaining, decorating and travelling. Lifestyle brands reinforce the social and economic hierarchies upon which narrowcasting rests, but they also promise to assist and enable TV viewers who aspire to membership in particular consumer communities.

Maureen Ryan traces the lifestyling of U.S. television to the launch of the Food Network and Home and Garden Television (HGTV) in the early 1990s. With these cable channels, Scripps, a conglomerate with publishing origins, transformed historically feminized domestic how-to formats and marginalized hobby programming into a successful "new way to hail niche audiences" (2015b, 60). Both the Food Network and HGTV circulated quasi-instructional blueprints for an idealized construction of the "good life," conveyed not only though seductive consumer imagery, but through forms of practical guidance, knowledge and advice offered under the rubric of their respective brands. In so doing, they established a template for other cable channels to insert television into multimedia lifestyle brands.

As Ryan points out, lifestyle channels (after some trial and error) avoided the dry and overtly pedantic conventions of earlier how-to and domestic programming. Instruction was fused with entertainment, and "aspirational and consumerist logics" borrowed from lifestyle magazines were harnessed to "consolidate viewership in a niche topic" as broadly as possible (2015b, 60). Programming was geared not only to TV viewers who wanted to learn how to redecorate a living room or prepare a new recipe, but those who aspired more broadly to the legitimated tastes, knowledges and lifestyles embodied by experts and hosts, or who found TV personalities like celebrity chef

Emeril Lagasse, the tough-talking host of Food Network's *How to Boil Water* (1993–), charismatic and fun to watch. By presenting domesticity as a zone for lifestyle formation and entertainment (as opposed to purely the site of women's work), cable networks invited men and women who worked outside the home to see themselves within Food Network and HGTV's brand communities. As one journalist observed at the time, dozens of new "lifestyle shows focused on the domestic arts—home repair, decorating, cooking, gardening, crafts, hobbies, pets and remodeling" were appealing to "millions of viewers," and not all of them housewives (quoted in Ryan 2015b, 42).

Lifestyle cable brands target women and, secondarily, men who are assumed to own their homes, have money to spend and invest in or aspire to the vision of the "good life" the brand represents. The TV viewer is addressed as an informal learner who will benefit from the knowledge and advice on offer. However, there is also an affective appeal to the vicarious pleasure of sumptuous food, furnishings, homes, tourist locations and other "desirable objects." Michael Newman's (2013) analysis of the tantalizing language and sensual camera close-ups deployed by Food Network's cooking programs (a style that is sometimes described as "food porn") can be extended to many lifestyle programs, from travelogues that fetishize natural scenery and bring exoticized images of faraway lands into the home, to fashion and decorating shows that use audible gasps and sighs to cast consumer objects as a source of corporeal pleasure and desire. The popularity of hybrid reality entertainment has come to bear on lifestyle programming as well, as evidenced by an increased focus on the personal lives of hosts and experts (Hollows 2003; Ryan 2015b), and the rise of hybrid games and competitions like *Top Chef* (2006–), *Cupcake Wars* (2009–2013) and *HGTV Star* (2006–2013), which minimize instruction and emphasize drama and suspense. And yet, lifestyle TV continues to trade on everyday pedagogies. Channels like HGTV and Food Network are differentiated from other brands of television by the promise of lifestyle instruction and advice, however pleasurable or informal the learning process may be (Newman 2013). Indeed, according to Binkley's definition, their success as lifestyle brands depends on taking the brand beyond the symbolic realm into everyday practices.

In guiding and facilitating these everyday practices, Scripps Interactive lifestyle brands exemplify Banet-Weiser's argument that the intensification of brand culture is more dynamic and complex than "excessive commercialism." Likewise, if brands have become main cultural contexts for "everyday living, individual identity, and affective relationships," as she suggests (quoted in Jenkins 2013), the lifestyling of television has a visible role in this process. Today, a growing number of cable networks are branded as lifestyle channels: the FYI Network (owned by A&E Networks, a joint subsidiary of Walt Disney Company and Hearst Corporation), Bravo (owned by NBCUniversal) and other channels. For a short time, there was a specialized cable network for people who liked fitness and exercise, Fit TV (owned by Discovery Communications), and a "green lifestyle" network, Planet Green (also owned by Discovery Communications), devoted to TV viewers interested in environmentally conscious living. When efforts to brand the viewing choices, interests, identities and everyday practices of niche markets are deemed commercial failures, rebranding is inevitable (Zimmerman 2015). The fact that some lifestyle brands fail reiterates the argument that branding is a dynamic (and potentially unsuccessful) *process* that involves the active participation of consumers (Arvidsson 2006).

Lifestyle brands cued to aspects of everyday living enable linkages between TV viewers and advertisers hoping to insert themselves into particular consumer clusters. For example, Home Depot sponsored the design show *Color Splash* (2007) and provides materials for many HGTV home renovation programs in exchange for integration into their content and scenes shot in the company's store. Because sponsors are welcomed into nonfiction narratives and the communities constituted around lifestyle channels, even the most egregious cases of product placement and integrated branding can appear natural and seamless (Deery 2012). The broadcast networks (ABC, CBS, NBC, Fox, CW) also connect commercial sponsors to the expertise and forms of belonging constructed around high-profile, primetime lifestyle programs aimed at a broad audience, as exemplified by Home Depot's visibility on *Extreme Makeover: Home Edition* (2002–2013) and the recurring role of Jello, Subway, Planet Fitness and other sponsors on *The Biggest Loser* (2004–). While broadcast networks use websites to promote their shows and advertisers, cable lifestyle brands use cross-promotional strategies to link TV viewers to branded content across media platforms.

For example, the HGTV brand operates across the cable network, several commercial websites, *HGTV* magazine, how-to books based on HGTV programs, social media platforms, and an extensive collection of licensed home products including flooring, bedding and paint supplies. Similarly, the Food Network brand encompasses the cable channel, *Food Network* magazine, websites, social media and branded merchandise such as Food Network cookware, knives and kitchen tools sold through retail venues as well as the Food Network's online store. When consumers are invited to follow multimedia brands across old and new media platforms, lifestyle branding is connected to the promise of participatory media culture (Jenkins 2006). Increasingly, TV viewers are encouraged to "participate" by tweeting, sharing, posting and interacting with lifestyle brands through phones, computers and other digital media. These activities cultivate brand loyalty, and they also help generate the substance and economic value of the brand. Some scholars see this activity as a form of "free labor" that blurs boundaries between production and consumption (Terranova 2000). This critique references the shift to an information-based postindustrial economy in which "economic value increasingly emerges less from tangible commodities" than from meanings and practices "structured through and around" brands (Lewis 2008, 147). Lifestyle brands are part of this shift, as their value rests less on any particular television program or product than on the social identities, meanings and expertise associated with the brand.

By using new technologies to interact with brand culture, viewers are said to "co-create" the sense of community and belonging that lifestyle channels package and sell. Activities like tweeting and visiting a show's website are increasingly tracked and used to sell loyal and engaged audiences to sponsors and advertisers as well. These activities also function as a grassroots type of marketing for cable channels. If the opportunity to "interact" with television promises an empowering alternative to passive consumption, it also enlists viewers to perform the work of "being watched" or making themselves visible to and productive for corporations, argues Mark Andrejevic (2004). Every time we interact with a television channel or its programs online or through social media, we are also helping to mine data about ourselves for market research. With each post, click and share, we actively contribute to the ever more refined forms of consumer profiling upon which niche marketing and branding depend.

The Bravo brand is at the forefront of efforts to enlist TV viewers as collaborators in niche marketing practices and the co-creation of brand value. Bravo was rebranded in 2003, the year it debuted *Queer Eye for the Straight Guy* (2003–2007), a reality makeover show that "reinvented the former

Figure 1.2 Bravo's TV personalities embody the attributes of its "affluencer" audience in this pitch to advertisers.

arts network into a lifestyle network focused on the show's five pillars of food, fashion, beauty, design and pop culture" (Hampp 2011). Deploying a psychographic approach to niche marketing based on assumptions about the "purchasing and lifestyle behavior" of its target viewers, Bravo constructed an audience profile of upscale, educated, trendsetting and tech-savvy women and gay men, and invented an identity—*affluencers*—to sell this lifestyle cluster to potential advertisers (Copple-Smith 2012, 291). According to *Adweek*, Bravo's affluencers were pitched as "the most affluent, educated, influential and engaged audience in cable." Passionate "about Bravo's buzzy content around food, fashion, beauty, design, digital and pop culture," they were said to be "super consumers" who "adopted new technologies," attended "movies on opening weekend," intended to "buy or lease new cars," and spent "more on personal care and household items" (*Adweek* 2012).

This promotional discourse, and the lifestyle cluster it invented, was given human form by Bravo programming. Following the network's rebranding, "real life" experts and personalities who displayed many of the characteristics attributed to Bravo affluencers were displayed across Bravo's lifestyle-themed reality shows. As Erin Copple-Smith (2012, 292) observes, from the cast members of the *Real Housewives* franchise (2006–) to *Millionaire Matchmaker* (2008–) Patti Stranger, female affluencers possessed "excellent or at least expensive taste, while male affluencers were embodied by the stylish and erudite *Project Runway* (2004–) mastermind Tim Gunn and the "well-groomed real estate moguls" of *Million Dollar Listing* (2006–). Perhaps no Bravo lifestyle personality embodies the affluencer identity more than celebrity fashion designer Rachel Zoe (*The Rachel Zoe Project*, 2008–2013). With a show that revolved around the manufacture of self-image and high-end consumption, Zoe's specialty was mediating the "masstige" market, a term used by marketers and Bravo executives to refer to the aspirations of mostly white, upper middle-class consumers newly interested in luxury items. "Maybe they can't afford the BMW, but they can swing the $400 Coach bag and certainly the $5 Starbucks latte," wrote the *New York Times* of these so-called affluencers (Dominus 2008).

Because Bravo programs share a "similar tone," they lend themselves to cross-promotional practices (such as having personalities from hit Bravo shows appear on other Bravo shows) that further solidify the channel's brand identity, says Copple-Smith (2012, 293). Bravo's promotion as a branded interface to a hip community of affluencers has also been conducive to synergistic corporate partnerships and integrated branding deals. Since 2003, products and brands have been woven into many Bravo lifestyle programs without apology. The *Rachel Zoe Project* (2008–2013), which revolved around celebrity stylist Rachel Zoe, integrated fashion houses, luxury products, designer clothing stores and online retailers such as Bluefly and Piperlime into storylines. The creative pursuits carried out on the fashion competition *Project Runway* involve Banana Republic, Macys, Neiman Marcus and other stores, while the design competition *Top Design* (2007–2008) has deals with Target and Swarovski. *Top Chef* integrates brands like Nestlé, Diet Dr. Pepper and Bombay Sapphire into cuisine challenges, and the Bravo program *Work of Art: The Next Great Artist* (2010–2011) had its contestants create artwork inspired by a ride in an Audi (Ward 2011).

As Henry Jenkins (2006) points out, integrated advertising is thought to be especially effective when it piggybacks on the affective ties that loyal TV viewers have with programs. This logic of "affective economics," in the language of marketers, extends to the Bravo network as a whole. Loyalty to the Bravo brand—encouraged by scheduling, programming, casting, cross-promotion and viewer interactivity—is assumed to spill over onto sponsors. Of course, products that resonate with the educated, affluent, trendsetting consumer clusters represented by the Bravo brand are more apt to enjoy this associative benefit. To date, the synergy between Bravo and its sponsors has been deemed highly effective: the imagined purchasing decisions and lifestyle behaviors of the so-called "affluencers" have been so seamlessly woven in to Bravo's reality and lifestyle offerings that in 2015 *Advertising Age* magazine named Bravo the "highest rated network for product placement effectiveness" in U.S. television (Ward 2011).

While the Bravo brand encompasses tie-in books and merchandise, the Web and social media are especially important to its robust multimedia brand community. Digital media technologies are harnessed to connect Bravo programming from "hot cuisine to haute couture" to TV viewers and Bravo personalities (called Bravolebrities), who live-tweet episodes and interact with fans through blogs and Facebook pages. Bravo has used Twitter so successfully to promote its programs and encourage fans to tweet with other fans and Bravolebrities that the network was nominated for a 2015 Shorty Award, the Oscars of the Twitter world, for "Best use of a Brand on Twitter." Referring to especially loyal fans as "brand ambassadors," Bravo enlists them to help spread the word about Bravo and its programs. "Our Bravo fans are so engaged with us on social, that we created @TheBravoholic," claims Bravo publicity. Each week, one fan gets to claim the handle and engage directly with "@Bravotv and the rest of the Bravo family on Twitter." The network also claims that its hashtags are so frequently promoted "on air, online and across social platforms," that they have become "a part of the everyday vernacular." Whether or not this is true, it is clear that the invitation to interact with the "Bravo family" of affluencers encourages TV viewers to align their identities and practices with the cable network. These activities generate "buzz" and bolster the brand value of Bravo as the meanings and sensibilities generated by fan practices are channeled into the trendsetting, savvy and upscale lifestyle it claims to enable and represent.

LIVING BRANDS

So far we have examined the branding of television networks geared to specialized lifestyle clusters, and the rise of lifestyle media brands that provide "frames of action" for everyday living and operate as interfaces to forms of consumer belong belonging organized around these lifestyles. These developments, which are both commercial and cultural, created the basic infrastructure for the explosion of lifestyle on U.S. television. There are other, more dispersed layers of branding at work in the lifestyling of television that warrant our attention as well. Across broadcast and cable channels, lifestyle experts and reality personalities operate as what Celia Lury calls "living brands" (2004, 77), and the settings for many unscripted series serve as backdrops for ambient forms of lifestyle branding and self-branding. These developments intersect with and perpetuate the rising celebrity status to the experts and the subjects of lifestyle and reality shows.

As Tania Lewis demonstrates, the proliferating number of lifestyle experts who now "introduce audiences to the rigors of self-care and lifestyle management" on television are increasingly treated as celebrities (2010, 580).

This marks a shift from the domestic and how-to programming of the pre-cable network era, when lifestyle experts may have achieved notoriety, but were not treated as celebrities. Nor did lifestyle experts build their own brands around their TV personas. While especially charismatic figures like Jack Lalanne, of the exercise program *The Jack Lalanne Show* (1951–1985), and Julia Child, host of *The French Chef* (1963–1973), achieved a degree of fame and engaged in book publishing, contemporary television has turned many lifestyle experts into celebrities who command media attention and use their television exposure to capitalize on their brand of expertise. With the expansion of the celebrity industry in the 1980s and the turn to life-style in the 1990s, experts offering guidance on cooking, home decorating, fashion, housekeeping, health, real estate, relationships, fitness and other dimensions of daily life have created lifestyle brands built around their TV personalities as much as their expertise.

Television has, in essence, facilitated a merger of celebrity culture and lifestyle expertise. The lifestyling of television has occurred alongside a rising impulse to attach celebrity to occupations that have not histori-cally been part of the entertainment complex: we now have celebrity chefs (Gordon Ramsay, Jamie Oliver), celebrity stylists (Rachel Zoe, Tim Gunn), celebrity fitness trainers (Jillian Michaels, Jackie Warner), celebrity doctors (Dr. Drew, Dr. Phil, Dr. Oz), celebrity "domestic goddesses" (Martha Stewart, Nigella Lawson) and even celebrity hairdressers (Tabatha Coffey, Kim Kimble), who have become famous through their appearances on life-style and reality programs. These TV experts embody a particular kind of celebrity status. They are not actors but "real people" who offer idealized skills, knowledge and expertise, while also projecting "ordinariness and attainability" (Bennett 2008). As Lewis points out, television's construction of intimacy and familiarity produces "personalities" rather than stars in the classic Hollywood sense (2010, 584), a tendency that is especially true of nonfiction and reality programming. An "intense emphasis on the familiar" imbues the lifestyling of television, from the everyday settings to the use of close-ups to the casting of real characters rather than fictional ones. The popularization of nonfiction and how-to lifestyle formats involved accen-tuating this sense of familiarity by placing more emphasis on the personal lives of experts and hosts. Celebrity lifestyle experts are sometimes filmed in their own homes (Hollows 2003; Ryan 2015a) and, even if they are not, they are increasingly shown as real people with interior lives. The familiarization of experts enables a fusion of detached expertise and embodied lifestyle, as lifestyle personalities simultaneously advise and "enact idealized domestic and personal lifestyles" (Lewis 2010, 587). By magnifying the personalities and everyday lives of lifestyle experts, television has made their new claim to celebrity possible.

Because lifestyle programming sells "ways of living and managing one's private life," experts with expertise in cooking, fashion, shopping, the body, mental health and other domains have been crucial to its expansion in recent decades. Likewise, when experts with "specific skill sets" achieve celebrity status, they become more valuable to lifestyle brands—including their own, Lewis observes. She cites the Martha Stewart Living Brand as a precursor to the rising tendency of lifestyle experts to not only endorse consumer products, but to produce "their own products and brand their own identities as lifestyle experts" (2010, 588). Celia Lury characterizes Stewart as the archetype of a "living brand" built around a celebrity (2004, 93). Stewart established a template for other lifestyle experts when she parlayed her expertise, and her television exposure, into a multimedia brand that encompasses books, magazines, more TV programs and digital media enterprises, as well as a line of kitchenware, hardware, craft supplies and home furnishings (Lewis 2010, 588). Oprah Winfrey is another early example of a living brand. While not an expert herself, Winfrey parlayed *The Oprah Winfrey Show*, a talk show that encouraged self-empowerment in the mold of her life trajectory and launched the careers of many lifestyle gurus, into a self-help empire that encompasses books, magazines and media appearances. More recently, Winfrey founded the cable channel OWN, branded as a cable "network of self-discovery, connecting people to each other and to their greatest potential," and which now serves as the hub of her multimedia lifestyle brand.

Created through the intimacy of television, living brands like Martha Stewart and Oprah give human form to lifestyle branding, and embody its capacity to extend beyond the fantasy of commodities into the everyday practices shaped through guidance, knowledge and advice (Binkley 2007a, 123). Since Stewart and Winfrey established their lifestyle brands in the early 1990s, it has become commonplace for lifestyle authorities to brand themselves across media platforms and launch expansive product lines that include DVDs, books and merchandise related to their personalized expertise. For example, Jillian Michaels, who achieved celebrity status through her role as a fitness trainer on The Biggest Loser, sells workout DVDs, self-help books, a weight loss app, coconut water, clothing and a meal plan for people who "want to lose weight and keep it off." Carson Kressley, the fashion expert on Queer Eye for the Straight Guy (2003–2007), has parlayed his exposure into regular gigs on other lifestyle programs such as The Chew (2011–) and How to Look Good Naked (2008–2010), as well as books, speaking engagements and a clothing line. Giada De Laurentiis, who secured celebrity status through her Food Network program Everyday Italian (2003–), sells books, DVDs, cookware, bakeware, and a line of pastas, spices and other Italian food items through a brand partnership with Target (Newman 2013). All of these TV personalities make use of the Web and social media to promote their lifestyle brands as an interface to lifestyle advice, resources, products and community.

Living brands exemplify what Lewis calls the commodification of lifestyle expertise, but their currency is more than naked commercialism. Following scholars like Lury and Banet-Weiser, we might think of TV's lifestyle experts as embodied interfaces to regimens for everyday living, shopping and self-fashioning. Through our intimate and familiar relationships with lifestyle personalities, we learn "who to be and how to live" within commercial frameworks. Experts, guides and mentors operate as personalized and, increasingly, monetized frames of action for achieving the aspirational identities and visions of good living that lifestyle television circulates. More broadly, the proliferation of living brands on television speaks to the intensification of brand culture writ large. Like brands of television and lifestyle brands, living brands reflect and contribute to the branding of all dimensions of social life, from institutions to expertise to education to relationships.

As reality entertainment has proliferated, it has generated another type of living lifestyle brand that does not hinge on expertise. Hybrid reality formats that follow real people in their natural environments have become launching pads for celebrities and unknown people alike to promote themselves as aspirational lifestyle brands. Less a Hollywood star than an "ordinary and relatable" TV personality, Kim Kardashian first captured the media spotlight when a sex tape in which she appeared was released on the Internet. She was catapulted to fame through her appearance on *Keeping Up With the Kardashians* (2007–) and other reality shows that chronicle the everyday lives of Kim and her co-stars, sisters Kourtney and Khloe, including *Kourtney and Kim Take New York* (2011–2012), *Kourtney and Kim Take Miami* (2009–2013) and *Kourtney and Khloe Take the Hamptons* (2014). Kardashian and her sisters appear often in the pages of tabloid magazines, where insatiable interest in their marriages, divorces, weight fluctuations, children's birthday parties and other happenings extends reality television's up-close engagement with their personal lives.

The Kardashian sisters have parlayed their television careers into a lucrative lifestyle brand that encompasses the Kardashian-owned Dash clothing retailer (billed as a "one stop contemporary women's boutique set to inspire the mindset of the confident, captivating, and charismatic women of today with an immaculate eye for fashion and style"), the Kardashian Kollection of women's clothing at Sears, jewelry, fragrances and beauty products (nail polish, makeup and hairstyling equipment). Storylines often revolve around these enterprises: as Maria Pramaggiore and Diane Negra point out, *Keeping Up With the Kardashians* is essentially a promotional device for Kardashian merchandise, spinoffs and endorsement deals, as Khloe Kardashian admitted when she called the show a "30-minute commercial" (2014, 85). The 2015 debut of *Dash Dolls*, a series revolving around the "trendy" employees of the Kardashian-owned clothing store, takes this promotional logic even further. While it is easy to dismiss the Kardashian shows as a giant product placement, brand culture is more complex than this (Banet-Weiser 2012).

Television also constructs the Kardashians as aspirational models for who to be and how to live. Unlike the lifestyle brands discussed so far, the Kardashian brand is not structured around professionalized skills or domestic expertise. While Kim has a series of how-to exercise videos, including *Fit In Your Jeans by Friday: Ultimate Butt Body Sculpt* (2009), *Butt Blasting Cardio Step* (2009) and *Amazing Abs Body Sculpt* (2010), and the sisters co-authored *Kardashian Konfidential* (2010), a book chock full of "advice and beauty tips," as well as heretofore unknown details about their personal lives, explicit instruction plays only a minor role in the monetization of the Kardashians. As Maria Pamaggore and Diane Negra point out (2014), the Kardashian brand is structured around the gendered embodiment of a glamorous lifestyle.

Keeping Up With the Kardashians takes its cues from earlier programs like *Lifestyles of the Rich and Famous* (1984–1995), which invited TV viewers to gape at the mansions, yachts, luxury cars and high-end socializing activities of socialites, business tycoons and celebrities. However, unlike that show, it closes the distance between TV viewers and the rich and famous by casting Kim and her sisters as characters, serializing their personal lives and taking TV viewers inside their "extraordinarily ordinary" experiences, relationships and emotions. This televisual intimacy has made it possible to construct an aspirational lifestyle brand around the Kardashians. Lury's concept of the living brand (2004) figures quite literally in this example, as the female bodies of the Kardashians are harnessed as "sexualized signifiers of social status and net worth" (Pramaggiore and Negra 2014, 85). The "luxury lifestyle and the lifestyle-enhancing products that the Kardashians sell," Pramaggiore and Negra observe, are "mediated through their rigidly gendered bodies and bodily display" (2014, 82). The Kardashians have also made use of social media platforms such as Twitter and Instagram to extend their branded personas and engage with TV viewers and fans directly.

By performing a version of themselves for commercial purposes, the Kardashians have perfected what critics call *self-branding*. Self-branding happens when personhood itself becomes a strategic activity, geared to profitmaking.

Figure 1.3 Kim Kardashian visits the lab that is manufacturing her new perfume on *Keeping Up With the Kardashians*.

Lifestyle experts increasingly brand their knowledge and expertise in ways that involve their "real life" identities and personal lives, as we have seen. Self-branding takes this a step further: individuals construct and perform personas that are explicitly brandable, so that the self becomes the commodity that is packaged and sold. Alison Hearn defines *self-branding* as a performance of identity geared to the generation of economic value (2008, 201) in which the individual produces his or her own "persuasive packaging." The idea that individuals can and should operate as brands has gained traction in the corporate sector in recent years—for example, downsized CEOs are urged to reinvent their personal brands and the unemployed are told to package themselves in terms that will "sell" in the marketplace. This logic is illustrated and extended on reality television, as participants are encouraged to "brand their own persona" for ratings, fame and economic rewards down the line (208). As Hearn points out, most reality TV participants work for free (or a small stipend) and are quickly forgotten once the shows are over. However, some have achieved a type of ordinary celebrity (Grindstaff 2011b) and have parlayed their exposure into commercial activity. These "success stories" encourage self-branding in reality television and society writ large.

The MTV reality program *The Hills* (2006–2010) is a case in point. Revolving around the lives of upscale young women in the Los Angeles area, *The Hills* brought lifestyle branding to a new level, and sent the message that non-famous "real people" could become celebrities through reality television. The show focused on Lauren Conrad and her circle of friends, narrating their friendships, romantic lives, social activities and internships in reality soap opera fashion. In the process, *The Hills* provided an ambient setting for lifestyle branding. As Elizabeth Affuso points out, much of the "real world" of the young women is determined by commercial partnerships: every trendy restaurant they visit, every item of designer clothing they wear, and even their career trajectories at companies like Epic Records and *Teen Vogue*, were chosen to advance the "needs of the brand that is being created" (2009). The "spectacular lives of the girls on *The Hills*" were also offered up as aspirational lifestyle templates, with TV viewers invited to "insert your 'self' here" (Hearn 2010, 68). While most TV viewers could not access their lavish California lifestyle or purchase the designer goods featured in the episodes, *The Hills* made extensive use of the Web to extend the opportunity to fashion oneself (at least vicariously) in the image of the characters. Under the slogan "Don't Just Watch it, Live it," the *Virtual Hills* Second Life platform invited fans to "create an avatar, interact with other viewers, the cast itself, and purchase products while pretending to live as Lauren and her friends to do" (Affuso 2009). MTV online also directed TV viewers to purchase less costly versions of the clothes, accessories and other accouterments of their lifestyle via partnerships with mall retailers.

To make all these commercial tie-ins work, *The Hills* needed its female characters to develop their own "person-character, image commodity or self-brand," argues Hearn. The performance of upscale young femininity enacted by Lauren and her friends was shaped by the aspirational tone of the program, its need for characters who would generate ratings, and its storytelling conventions and sponsorship narratives (2010, 68). The cast members, however, also monetized their branded performances for their own commercial gain, through media appearances, pop albums, spinoffs and merchandising deals. Conrad launched a clothing line and penned a bestselling book, *L.A. Candy*. "The young women on *The Hills* are models of models, offering their lives up week after week to the MTV cameras, becoming profitable self-brands and modeling how effective self-branding might be done," their lives serving as "extended promotions for the MTV network and their own celebrity brand," Hearn suggests (2010, 68). *The Hills*, she says, instructed a generation of TV viewers and reality show participants about the branding of the self.

Following *The Hills*, a number of lifestyle-themed reality programs have provided launching pads for ordinary celebrities to establish brands, including Bravo's *Real Housewives* franchise, which generates soap opera narratives from the real lives of wealthy women in several cities across the US When feminist critic Betty Friedan diagnosed "the problem that has no name," housewives were confined to the family home. On Bravo, "real-life" housewives are enlisted as amateur performers who use television to perpetuate their ordinary celebrity, entrepreneurial activities and personal brands. *Real Housewives of New York*, and other versions of the program set in Orange County, Miami, Atlanta and New Jersey, invite TV viewers to identify with the emotional ups and downs of women who live an aspirational lifestyle displayed through luxurious settings, designer goods and lavish spending

(Cox and Proffitt 2012). The characters must perform typecast versions of themselves that resonate with the programs' emphasis on personal conflict and the emotional upheaval in the personal lives of the glamorous and well-to-do. Yet, many cast members have also exploited these commercial personas to brand themselves as aspirational lifestyle authorities (Arcy 2015). Housewives use their television exposure and social media platforms to bolster their fame and promote jewelry, wine, skin care products, cookbooks, restaurants, shape wear and clothing lines. These entrepreneurial activities are also woven in to the program's narratives. Bethenny Frankel, who appears on *Real Housewives of New York*, and the spinoffs *Bethenny Getting Married* (2010) and *Bethenny Ever After* (2010–2012), used her TV persona to establish her successful Skinnygirl cocktail line and develop a lifestyle brand encompassing bestselling self-help books on romance, dieting and other topics, an exercise DVD, a website and a (now cancelled) talk show.

While self-branding has grown pervasive in reality television, characters on factual programs revolving around affluent lifestyles seem to be most brandable. Programs that invite TV viewers to emotionally identify with the experiences of "real people" who populate lavish and luxurious worlds are especially valuable as launching pads for entrepreneurial activities and the monetization of TV personas. This is not surprising, for the layers of branding at work in the lifestyling of television tend to equate profitability—and the "good" life—with upscale or aspirational consumer clusters. Brands of television target consumers only if they are attractive to advertisers and capable of generating brand value. Likewise, lifestyle brands operate as interfaces to tastes and identities that promise inclusivity, but often perpetuate class hierarchies, gender norms and racial inequalities. Living brands, meanwhile, connect templates for living to marketable forms of personhood. Brand culture provides the commercial scaffolding for the lifestyling of television—but it doesn't fully explain it. As we will see in later chapters, the turn to lifestyle intersects with a range of social and political pressures that both resonate with and sometimes contradict the intensified logic of branding.

2

THE SELF AS PROJECT

In June 2015, Fox News posed the question "Are TV makeover shows bad for us?" Although the makeover concept has been a staple of lifestyle and reality programming for some time, the debut of three new "style-centric shows," scheduled back to back on the TLC cable network, presented a timely occasion to revisit a trend that shows little sign of abating. The programs under discussion were *Love, Lust or Run* (2015–), which claims to "help women who are lost in their style choices," *Brides Gone Styled* (2015–), which revamps "worst-dressed brides," and *Dare to Wear* (2015–), in which two participants swap wardrobes to "experience what life is like donning a totally different fashion style." Some commentators interviewed for the Fox story condemned the new shows for perpetuating a superficial obsession with fashion and style, and pointed out that the "shimmering final appearances" featured on makeover programs are unattainable for most people. Women and girls, they noted, are especially vulnerable to illusory standards of perfection because they are judged more on their looks than men. Other commentators were much more optimistic, claiming that makeover programs inspire and empower people to "feel better about themselves." The journalist concluded that, whatever critics think, the shows "resonate" with TV viewers, as evidenced by strong ratings. Tellingly, for a cable brand known for advocating free market capitalism, the takeaway was that makeovers are here to stay, because "style sells" (Johnson 2015).

Why does style sell? More to the point, why is so much unscripted television devoted to guiding and improving the way people dress—and eat, decorate, shop and even date—and what do these programs suggest about contemporary society? Fox News did not explore these complicated questions, implying instead that consumer demand is simply responsible for the enduring makeover trend. The assumption that TV viewers are in control of what we see on television conceals the profit-maximizing practices of the TV industry. As we saw in earlier chapters, popular nonfiction and reality programs are often cheaper to produce than news and fictional entertainment, and present ample occasion for product placement and integrated branding. However, commercialism can't fully explain television's preoccupation with stylizing and transforming people and their environments. We must also consider how wider social, economic and political discourses and pressures come to bear on programming trends. The simplistic debate over positive versus negative messages regurgitated by Fox News cuts short this type of analysis. This chapter does not resolve once and for all whether makeover shows are good or bad, but considers the presentation of the *self as project* across a wide range of lifestyle and reality television. The style makeover is one example of a plethora of formats that engage and assist with processes of self-making and lifestyle formation (Palmer 2004, 2008). To understand why these programs are so abundant now, I situate television's impetus to shape and transform the self within the conditions of late modern capitalist societies.

TLC's new slate of makeover programs may well perpetuate beauty and gender norms, but the shows also claim to solve problems arising from fashion "mistakes," reflect on multiple ways of dressing and living, and empower participants—and by extension TV viewers—to navigate a burgeoning maze of consumer options and lifestyle choices. In that sense, they convey the idea that the self is less a fixed entity than a self-made project that involves a high degree of reflexivity, strategy and attention. Social theorists explain the imperative to approach the self as project to intersecting factors, including the decline of traditional ways of life, the postwar expansion of the college-educated middle classes, the growth of therapeutic culture, and the shifting economic and political conditions of late modern capitalist societies (Bell and Hollows 2005; Lewis 2008). While scholars debate the degree to which these developments have truly eroded traditional structures of identity and replaced them with an imperative to "choose how we construct our identities through lifestyle practices" (Bell and Hollows 2005, 3), the assumption that the self can—and must—be perpetually worked on, styled and transformed is perpetuated by popular discourse, the media, advertising and the self-help industry. The lifestyling of television is part of this mediated culture of the perpetually made, constantly reflecting self. With the expansion of popular nonfiction and reality formats in recent decades, television has become an especially visible "cultural technology" (Bennett 1998) for fashioning ourselves as subjects.

As Katherine Sender points out, the presumed "unfixing" of the self in late modern capitalist societies reframes social identity as a proliferating array of individual choices about what to wear, how to live, what to eat and who to be. The purpose of lifestyle television, she suggests, is to assist TV viewers in navigating this "puzzling diversity of possibilities" (2012, 17). From cooking and home shows to makeovers and competitions, lifestyle-themed television presumes the freedom—and imperative—to create our own life trajectories and circulates resources (advice, instruction, templates) for aestheticizing, managing and transforming our wardrobes, bodies, homes, palates, psyches, behaviors and relationships. While the tutelary nature of much lifestyle and reality programming suggests that anyone can partake in self-fashioning, the templates and guidelines offered tend to reinscribe social hierarchies in the language of self-actualization, empowerment and individual "choice." As we will see, lifestyle and reality television has become especially useful to a governing logic that expects everyone to be "entrepreneurs of the self" (Rose 1992) who maximize their everyday choices, and manage their own fates and fortunes, regardless of circumstances. The paradox of lifestyle TV is that it tethers the promise of individual freedom to decide "who to be and how to live" (Giddens 2001) to the advice of lifestyle experts and the agendas of authorities.

AESTHETICIZING EVERYDAY LIFE

The programming examined in this book contributes to what scholars call a shift from "ways of life to lifestyle" (Chaney 1996, 2000). According to David Chaney, a way of life is associated with the shared norms, rituals and patterns of stable communities and institutions grounded in "distinctive and specifiable localities" (2000, 82). Geographical mobility, the decline of manufacturing in the West, and media and consumer culture are said to have "unfixed" traditional ways of life and fostered a self-conscious approach to identity and lifestyle. In the late modern era, the self has become a "reflexive project, for which the individual is responsible," explains Anthony Giddens. While critics contest the assumption that individuals—especially those marginalized by gender, race, class and sexual orientation—are free to determine their sense of themselves and place in the world, few would dispute the seductive pervasiveness of the message "We are not what we are, but what we make of ourselves" (Giddens 1991, 75).

Social theorists do not suggest that identity has become a "free for all." While everyone is called upon to participate, the pursuit of reflexive self-fashioning is constrained by "differential access to forms of self-actualization and empowerment" (Giddens 1991, 6). The demise of traditional ways of life has also occurred in tandem with the rise of mechanisms for shaping appropriately "self-reflexive" subjects. Ulrich Beck describes the "disembedding and re-embedding of industrial society ways of life by new ones in which individuals must produce, stage and cobble together their biographies themselves" as a process of *individualization* (1994, 15). Consumer culture and popular media are technologies of individualization, to the extent that they circulate a "repertoire of styles" that individuals are encouraged to "monitor and adapt" for themselves (Chaney 2000, 81). Lifestyle television plays an especially visible role in the process of individualization by offering TV viewers an assortment of customizable templates, models and resources for "choosing" and assembling their identities and lifestyles. The Food Network's cooking/lifestyle program *Pioneer Woman* (2011–), hosted by Ree Drummond, exemplifies the disembedding and re-embedding of identity much as Beck describes.

Drummond is a college-educated, former city-dwelling career woman who adopted a rural lifestyle when she married a cattle rancher, quit her job and relocated to Oklahoma to become a full-time wife and mother. The show revolves around the everyday details of her chosen lifestyle: attending church picnics, riding horses, tending to her husband and family, preparing "all-American" meals for the Drummond clan and workers on the ranch. While Drummond embodies an agrarian way of life and a traditional model of femininity based on the primacy of the nuclear family and the sexual division of labor in the home, however, her biography and lifestyle were not inevitable or predetermined—they are presented as the result of *her own self-stylization and reflexive choices*. As a rule, lifestyle television similarly constructs personhood and everyday life as a reflexive choice.

The chaos associated with late modernity, in which "identities are torn apart and made fluid," is channeled into new ways of fixing identity, argues Sam Binkley. Experts are crucial to this process. Tania Lewis argues that the "stylization of life" has required a visible expansion of cultural intermediaries. Drawing from the sociologist Pierre Bourdieu, she traces the explosion of lifestyle guides, tastemakers and aesthetic gurus on television to the aspirational culture of self-expression and continual self-improvement associated with the expanding middle classes. Experts "offering (or selling) their own art of living as an example to others" are central to this set of skills and competencies, she contends (2008, 9). Recent decades have seen a proliferation of lifestyle experts offer templates for living and guide consumers on how to make choices in an expanding array of spheres, from food and fashion to travel and exercise (Binkley 2007b, 77). Lifestyle TV addresses

Figure 2.1 Ree Drummond demonstrates her rural lifestyle choices on *Pioneer Woman*.

a "DIY self" (Lewis 2008, 5), but it simultaneously offers expert instruction and advice to help alleviate the anxieties generated by the imperative
to create oneself through acts of choice. The expansion of how-to lifestyle
programming, enabled by the proliferation of cable channels, tethers individualization to perpetual reliance on experts.

As we have seen in previous chapters, purely instructional, skill-oriented
programs that teach TV viewers how to cook a roast or remodel a house
have given way to formats that infuse lifestyle instruction with entertainment appeals and the pleasure of vicarious consumption (Newman 2013).
Programs presented on cable lifestyle brands like HGTV and the Food
Network often combine informal pedagogy with the display and expert
discussion of sumptuous food, aestheticized environments and stylish furnishings. They mediate repertoires of styles and provide informal guidance,
often embodied by the host and inscribed in studio and on-location settings,
on questions of who to be and how to live. Identity is presented in part as
the result of consumer choices that must be calibrated to match the person
we think we are, or would like to be. A case in point is the property show
in which experts (decorators, realtors) help ordinary people "aestheticize
everyday home life in connection with distinct identities" (McElroy 2008,
quoted in White 2014, 390). This can involve renovation, redecorating and
landscaping an existing home, or buying a new one. As Mimi White points
out, shows like *House Hunters* (1999–) do not provide technical instruction
on purchasing a home. Instead, they enable and guide a quest to match
property with identities and lifestyles. In addition to exploiting the "appeal
of looking at other people's domiciles and seeing what different kinds of
property look like," these shows link the expression of one's identity to self-
reflexive consumption. As White explains, "Whether participants are trying
to buy a home or sell one and move to another, they are all looking for the
place that is just right for them" (2014, 390).

The idea that a home should express the individuality and style of its
owner speaks to the "aestheticization of everyday life" in postindustrial
societies. Mike Featherstone (1991) argues that the postwar expansion
of the educated middle classes upset traditional social hierarchies and put
questions of identity into flux. From the upwardly mobile emerged a new
consumer sensibility marked by an especially "stylized awareness" of the

process of consumption. As traditional class distinctions blurred, the new middle classes turned to consumer culture to convey their emerging social position (Lury 2011, 53). This was not about copying the cultural tastes of social elites, but to do with adopting a reflexive approach to consumption itself: "Rather than unreflexively adopting a lifestyle, through tradition or habit, the new heroes of consumer culture make lifestyle a life project and display their individuality and sense of style in the particularity of the assemblage of goods, clothes, practices, experiences, appearance and bodily dispositions they design together into a lifestyle," Featherstone explains (1991, 86). Like the nineteenth-century dandy who "makes of his body, his behavior, his feelings and passions, his very existence, a work of art," the new middle classes embraced an aesthetic approach to life, which has become pervasive within consumer culture as a whole (1991, 67). Lifestyle television illustrates and enables this aesthetic approach to daily life, translating the desire for distinctive identity into a never-ending process of conscious lifestyle design.

Lifestyle programs tend to address consumer clusters imagined as upscale or aspiring to upper middle-class identities and lifestyles. However, as Frances Bonner points out, even niche cable brands must appeal beyond this small population. For this reason, she argues, the "fantasies on offer are presented in as inclusive a way as possible" (2003, 131). The assumption that, because identity is flexible, virtually anyone can potentially achieve the models of the "good life" demonstrated on television, is part of this discourse of inclusion.

Another way to cultivate a broad audience for niche programs is to bring ordinary people (often coded as working or lower class) into the mix as subjects of transformation. Makeover programs like *Brides Gone Styled*, which operates on the premise that some bridal gowns are unquestionably "tacky," tend to perpetuate a social hierarchy of taste. As the sociologist Pierre Bourdieu (1984) has shown, aesthetic choices are related to the social structures of everyday life as experienced by different classes— what he calls the habitus. In other words, our social position shapes our "choices," which are not valued equally by society. Working-class aesthetic tastes, Bourdieu notes, are usually discredited as unsophisticated and vulgar. Makeover shows suggest that anyone can potentially acquire "better" taste by consulting and emulating knowledgeable experts, thereby partially disrupting the notion that social hierarchies are inevitable or fixed. However, as Helen Wood and Beverly Skeggs point out, the idea that we can all choose to "better" ourselves and our daily environments is ultimately another way of perpetuating class hierarchies. "Choice mediates taste, displaying the success and failure of the self to make itself," they write, alluding to the extent to which those who fail to transform themselves using the templates and resources that television makes so widely available have no one but themselves to blame for their maligned class status (2004, 206). Even privileged consumers, however, cannot rest assured in their tastes when class identity is understood to require *ongoing* self-stylization and a permanent reliance on experts. As Featherstone points out, the aestheticization of everyday life speaks in part to the role of education in upward mobility, and a perceived need to be "continuously learning and enriching oneself" felt most acutely by the new middle classes (1991, 48). When this disposition extends into self-fashioning, taste becomes a perpetual project.

Featherstone acknowledges that this "new consumer sensibility" is contradictory, as it hinges on a conflict between self-actualization pursued through productive forms of learning and the pursuit of pleasure through "expressive and liberated" lifestyles (Lury 2011, 96). This mirrors an older tension between the Protestant work ethic (Weber 1992), which posited that "self-improvement is to be achieved through rational and disciplined work," and the "self-actualization, expressivity, hedonism, and aesthetics" associated with the Romantic ethic (Lears 1983; Campbell 1987; Maguire 2008, 113). According to Featherstone, this tension is managed through a type of "calculated hedonism" in which individuals move "into and out of control" of their choices, enjoying the clash between the pleasure of unconstrained consumption and the discipline required of self-cultivation (Lury 2011, 96). Lifestyle TV similarly negotiates the tension by fusing consumption and pedagogy, work and fun, fantasy and reflexive self-making. By combining entertainment and instruction, lifestyle programs are able to incorporate both sides of the new consumer sensibility.

The Bravo cable brand is especially synchronized to calculated hedonism. While Bravo reality shows are rarely didactic or overtly instructional, they do revolve around food, fashion, shopping and other lifestyle domains.

Moreover, Bravo programs often celebrate luxury and conspicuous consumption. The *Rachel Zoe Project* (2008–2013), which revolves around celebrity stylist Rachel Zoe, presents a revolving parade of designer dresses, jewelry and shoes, lovingly filmed and discussed at length by the participants. The *Real Housewives* franchise (2006–) profiles the daily lives of spoiled wealthy women who love to shop. *Million Dollar Listing* (2006–) takes TV viewers inside luxury condos and sumptuous mansions. The *Millionaire Matchmaker* (2008–) caters to the dating needs of rich clients who drive sports cars and dine at trendy upscale restaurants. However, Bravo also encourages an ironic response to these characters and scenarios—what is sometimes called the "Bravo wink." The ironic sensibility associated with the Bravo brand allows TV viewers to simultaneously lose themselves in vicarious luxury consumption and distance themselves from the people on screen by poking fun at them. The Bravo wink doesn't exactly replicate the push and pull between the pursuit of pleasure and the perceived need for more productive forms of self-realization that a quasi-instructional or how-to program would. However, as a viewing disposition, the Bravo wink does alleviate some of the anxiety generated by conspicuous consumption and the presumably lowbrow pleasure of reality entertainment as a whole.

The aestheticization of everyday life also intersected with the intensification of niche marketing discussed in previous chapters. The fragmentation of the consumer market to create more specialized consumer divisions, as exemplified by the rise of gourmet food and designer goods, made stylizing and customizing everyday life through consumption more possible for people with sufficient economic resources. The desire to identify and target specialized consumer clusters also led marketers to commodify "authentic" experiences, such as international travel, as another aestheticized resource for identity formation. In the 1970s, according to Sam Binkley, VALS psychographic research identified a tension between two value systems, "one endorsing the individualism, competition and acquisitiveness of mainstream American society and another stressing the expressiveness, ease with oneself, and earnestness associated with youth and counterculture" (2007b, 98). The latter value system was associated with college-educated professionals of the postwar generation—members of the new middle classes discussed by Featherstone—who were deemed "self-expressive, individualistic, concerned with people, impassioned, diverse, complex." To research this "vanguard group," marketers believed they must find a way to connect "deeper meanings" to consumer choices. The consumption of goods, however self-consciously stylized, was no longer enough: as "experiencers," the professionals of the new middle classes craved "intense transforming moments" and self-improvement through "indulging in new experiences." As this desire was commodified and sold back to "experiencers" longing for authenticity, it became part of the burgeoning culture of the self as mediated through consumer practices (2007b, 98). Television similarly trades on vicariously meaningful, intense and transforming experiences, as exemplified by a cadre of lifestyle programs on the Travel Channel and the Discovery Channel—including *Anthony Bourdain: No Reservations* (2005–2012) and *Survivorman* (2004–)—which take TV viewers to exotic places and extreme situations.

While theorists like Featherstone seem optimistic about the aestheticization of everyday life, other critics are skeptical. As Celia Lury (2011) points out, the creative and stylized approach to consumption associated with the middle classes is rarely ascribed to working-class consumers. Makeover programs (which often target subordinated classes) suggest a ratcheting up of the demands of self-reflexivity—and an intensification of the expectation that "individuals respond to what is reflected back to them" (2011, 28). The long-running makeover program *What Not to Wear* (2003–2013) takes the creativity and pleasure out of consumption altogether, and deploys surveillance, shaming and strict fashion rules, which subjects are expected to master under the tutelage of experts and later enforce on themselves. After a harsh initial evaluation by the hosts, participants are offered advice for transforming their appearances—and their lives—through a wardrobe upgrade. They are sent shopping for new clothes to complete this mission, while hidden cameras capture their every move. Their purchases are then scrutinized by the hosts, who decide whether they are appropriate, flattering and conducive to the "better" self-image suggested by the experts and agreed upon in advance. For many of the subjects, the process is humiliating and stressful—not pleasurable or playful.

As Lury notes, the "mythical figure of the abnormal consumer" further reveals the white male privilege associated with the prototypical dandy and legitimated forms of stylized consumption and calculated hedonism today. Reality shows about shopping addictions (*My Shopping Addiction*, 2012–) and hoarding (*Hoarders*, 2009–2013; *Hoarding: Buried Alive*, 2010–2013; *Hoarders: Family Secrets*, 2015–) often cast their female, working-class and African American participants as pathological consumers who are unable to navigate the competing ethics of productivity and pleasure, gratification and restraint.

Advice programs and interventions that claim to help people get out of debt often blame individuals for overindulging. When MTV launched its "Indebted" campaign to control massive debt accumulation among college students at the height of the financial crisis in 2010, it circulated images of conspicuous consumers who spent their student loan money on Spring Break vacations and designer lattes, implicitly blaming youth for the student loan crisis. Reality programs like *True Life* (1998–) integrated similar messages into profiles of indebted young people, and classic rap and hip hop videos were replayed with "pop up" captions calling into question the spending choices associated with an African American "bling" lifestyle. And yet, as Diane Negra points out, when marginalized subjects pursue alternative consumer practices to survive unemployment and manage financial uncertainties, they are treated ambivalently (2013). The working-class women of *Extreme Couponing* (2010–2012), who amass and redeem large quantities of grocery store coupons, are not cast as clever, creative or heroic, but as obsessive and bizarre. As these examples suggest, the freedom and flexibility associated with the late modern self is not afforded to everyone equally: "The argument that all are much freer to acquire the lifestyle—and thus the identity—of their choice," Lury notes, "runs the risk of slipping into an imaginary world of equal appearances, and thus of becoming a rhetoric that all are equal, even if some remain more equal than others" (2011, 197).

ETHICS AND CARE OF THE SELF

Lifestyle television's engagement with the self as project is not limited to the aestheticizing of identity through consumer choices. Everyday behaviors, habits, attitudes and practices are also examined, problematized and presented as reflexive ethical choices. The "loosening" of fixed identities (Binkley 2007b) has coincided with the growth of "everyday experts of subjectivity"

(Hawkins 2001, 413) and the proliferation of mediated resources (self-help books, magazines, apps, websites, TV programs) for monitoring, reflecting upon and cultivating ourselves across spheres of everyday life. From dating shows and makeovers to boot camps and rehab programs, lifestyle and reality television problematizes conduct with an eye toward ethical reflection and improvement. A large number of programs examine ways to live, offer tutorials in care and management of the self, and circulate techniques and regimens for everyday living that can be adopted and customized (Hawkins 2001, 412; Ouellette and Hay 2008). Competitions, docusoaps, life "swapping" programs and other forms of reality entertainment may not offer explicit instruction, but they do encourage TV viewers to "reflect on ways of being," and evaluate the lives and conduct of others (Hawkins 2001, 412). As Annette Hill points out, the practical and moral instruction of lifestyle programs is not limited to "external advice on how to improve our home, or our appearance." We are also presented "internal advice on how to improve our relationship with ourselves" (2007, 121). Putting this another way, Gay Hawkins argues that expert advice is never purely technical: it is also ethical because it privileges "certain conducts over others," and endorses techniques for relating to and cultivating ourselves in relation to "implicit moral problematizations" (2001, 418).

Michel Foucault refers to this concern with how to live as *ethics*. Ethics for Foucault does not refer to a strict moral code (thou shall not do this or that), but to the "relationship one ought to have with oneself," and the guidelines one sets for "conducting oneself in the world of one's everyday existence" (Rose 1996, 135). Theorists use the term "care of the self" to refer to the ethical process of attending to ourselves as subjects, which entails reflecting upon and accounting for our thoughts, behaviors, experiences, actions, habits and relationships, often through personal writing, mentorship, tutorials and practical exercises. While Foucault focused on the ethical practices of privileged white men in Antiquity, scholars have extended his framework to make sense of how individuals in the late modern era constitute themselves through self-conscious ethical processes (Ouellette and Arcy 2015). Foucault (1980, 1984, 1997) has been helpful for developing an understanding of subjectivity that accounts for the active and ongoing involvement of individuals, while also recognizing that identity is socially constructed within uneven societal contexts. Foucault's concept of "techno-logies of the self" is especially relevant for understanding the self as project. Technologies of the self, he argued, are practices, or methods, that "permit individuals to effect by their own means or with the help of others a certain number of operations on their own bodies and souls, thoughts, conduct, and way of being, so as to transform themselves in order to attain a certain state of happiness, purity, wisdom, perfection, or immorality." The details of these actions and practices are the basis of the self, Foucault suggested, because "they are you—what you thought, what you felt" (1988, 29).

Technologies of the self are never practiced in a vacuum. As Foucault explained, if the subject constitutes himself in "active fashion, by practices of the self, these practices are nevertheless not something that the subject invents by himself." Rather, they are "patterns that he finds in his culture and which are proposed, suggested and imposed on him by his culture, his society and his social group" (1997, 291). Today, we are bombarded with all manner of advice about who to be and how to live through advertis-ing, film, magazines, digital media, and nonfiction and reality television. Institutions and experts also play a role in "making up" people. Fields like psychology and social work—what Nikolas Rose (1998) calls the "psy complexes"—help construct normative models of healthy personhood and everyday living, and provide techniques for assessment, evaluation and modification.

Lifestyle TV is flooded with psy experts, including psychiatrists, thera-pists, self-esteem gurus and counselors. Some of these authorities, including Philip McGraw (Dr. Phil, 2002–) and Robert Drew (Celebrity Rehab, 2008–) have become TV celebrities who parlay their exposure into lucrative self-help brands. Many makeover programs borrow from the psy complexes to cast experts and hosts as pseudo-counselors who diagnose and fix alleged problems of self-esteem and crises of the will lurking beneath the surface of external concerns (Sender 2012). Programs like What Not to Wear (2003–2013), How to Look Good Naked (2008–2010) and Mission Makeover (2009–) draw from the psy complexes to problematize and improve the relationship that participants have with themselves, in addition to teaching them how to improve their physical appearances. The burgeoning self-help indus-try, geared to overcoming inner problems and achieving health, romance, happiness, wealth and professional success, is also well represented on life-style-themed programming. The self-help authorities who circulate on television may not have formal membership in the psy complex (many are not credentialed professionals), but they popularize its techniques and translate the project of the self into step-by-step plans for reflecting upon and altering self-perceptions, habits, behaviors and choices. Self-help experts sometimes adopt the detached and authoritative demeanor of psychologists and social workers, but more often than not they forge intimate connections and emotional alliances with the subjects they claim to assist and empower. The OWN Network, operated by Oprah Winfrey (who launched the careers of many TV psy experts), is branded as a channel for self-actualization and features a large number of programs that combine psy expertise with a more intimate approach to self-care, including the signature show Fix My Life (2012–).

Even more than psy experts, lifestyle TV relies on a plurality of lifestyle experts who open up the intimate zones of daily life for ethical reflection and make recommendations on everything from sex to body image to mental and physical health. Lifestyle experts are often personable figures whose authority is based as much on their private experience as their diplomas. The ordinary people who appear on many lifestyle and reality shows also reflect on personhood and everyday life, and share technologies of the self in a wide range of settings, from high-stakes competitions to docusoaps. The lifestyling of television has created a mediated platform for an intimate approach to care of the self to unfold. Foucault uses the term care of the self to refer to ethical frameworks for "living a beautiful life" and caring for the self as a matter of pleasure, autonomy and self-mastery that flourished in ancient times. The self was not "given" nor governed by universal laws, but cultivated and regulated through daily choices and practices that received endless reflection and attention. In this milieu, everyday life took on an "aesthetics of existence"—the individual was akin to a work of art, to the extent that care of the self involved a "principle of stylization of conduct for those who wished to give their existence the most graceful and accomplished form possible" (1985, 250–251). This was not about consuming goods, but about reflecting upon everyday practices involving food, sexuality, exercise, the body and relationships with others, keeping meticulous records about these matters and consulting with mentors, with the goal of living the best way possible. While Foucault realized that ethical judgments (e.g. what is considered "best") are historically bound, he envisioned affinities between ancient technologies of the self and the cultivation and care of the self in late modern societies. With the declining influence of traditional ways of life, and the waning of institutions and rigid rules governing sexuality, morality and everyday life, the twentieth century opened up new "freedoms and challenges" for subjects to fashion themselves and their lives in ethical ways (Gauntlett 2008, 142).

Sam Binkley traces the mainstreaming of the care of the self to an "intimate discourse of lifestyle" that gained currency in the 1970s. In the wake of the social movements and youth countercultures of the 1960s, new lifestyle experts appeared to mediate "personal becoming." The search for alternatives to mainstream society and mass culture gave rise to an alternative lifestyle print culture through which mediators circulated ethical advice and resources for creating new ways of everyday living. The new lifestyle experts, who were part of the alternative cultures they advised, published pamphlets, catalogs, books and articles on topics ranging from solar energy and organic food to sexuality and yoga. Unlike traditional experts, whose authority hinged on university credentials and "abstract pedagogy," they spoke in a "warm and personal" voice, and guided others on the basis of "intimate knowledge, the kind that can only be gained from direct experience, learning and personal growth in one's life" (2007b, 79). They developed an ethic of care in the sense theorized by Foucault, Binkley suggests, in which new questions about who to be and how to live were paramount.

As marketers devised ways to target nascent lifestyle clusters who valued "authentic" ways to develop themselves to the "fullest extent of their capacities" (Binkley 2007b, 93) over stylized consumption, the new model of "caring expertise" was folded into mainstream media and consumer culture (2007b, 78–79). In the process, what had been a collective practice of ethical reflection and self-making became individualized. By the 1980s, this privatized version of care of the self was evidenced in the rise of commercial lifestyle experts like Jane Fonda, whose instructional voice collapsed "knowing, doing and personal being into an intimate mode of address," and who claimed to care about the women she advised (2007b, 81). Many of the lifestyle experts we see on television today are cut in the same mold. Claiming intimate knowledge, and speaking to participants and TV viewers in an affective and encouraging way, these modern-day guides bring an ethic of caring into a strand of television pervaded by stylized consumption, consumer hierarchies, sales pitches and brands.

Gay Hawkins points to TV chef Jamie Oliver (The Naked Chef, 1999–2001; Jamie at Home, 2007–2008; Jamie Oliver's Food Revolution, 2010–2011; Jamie's 30-Minute Meals, 2010) as an example. Frequently filmed at home with his family, and constructed as passionate about improving the quality of every-day eating and educating the public on issues of nutrition, Oliver connects everyday ethics to an intimate mode of expertise. On his shows, cooking is more than a skill or a way to express identity; it is a site from which to explore "modes of living and self-cultivations." Learning "how to fillet a fish, or scramble an egg is not just a lifestyle matter, it is about the production of . . . personal habits, attitudes and rituals that are informed by ethical values and principles," says Hawkins (2001, 418). The (now defunct) Planet Green cable network is another example of how the ethical dispositions and alternative self-care regimens discussed by Binkley are mainstreamed on lifestyle-themed television. Planet Green programs revolved around challenges and experiments designed to encourage ethical reflection on one's impact on the environment. Programs included Living with Ed (2007–2010), which profiled actor Ed Begley Jr.'s "low impact, environmentally conscious" lifestyle, and Wa$ted (2007), a show where green lifestyle experts confronted "average households about their long-term impacts on the environment," to encourage reflection on the environmentalism of everyday choices. While Planet Green was rebranded and its successor no longer encourages environmentalism, Pivot TV, a cable network geared to "socially conscious millennials," has picked up this theme with shows like Human Resources (2014), which follows a group of young people who are committed to reducing landfill waste by turning garbage into useful objects and teaching others to do the same.

The mainstreaming of a caring ethic can also be seen in the proliferation of reality shows about the tiny house movement (Tiny House, Big Living, 2014– ; Tiny House Builders, 2014– ; Tiny House Hunters, 2014– ; Tiny House Nation, 2014–). In these programs, people who have self-consciously chosen to downsize their lives challenge other people to give up "wide open spaces" and sprawling suburban homes for smaller, less expensive and more sustainable living arrangements. As with Planet Green programming, these "intimate experts," and the lifestyles they embody and advocate, are mediated by entertainment conventions and packaged to deliver suspense, emotion and drama in the interests of ratings. In the US, television's priority is to maximize profit through branding, sponsorship and advertising. The exploration of everyday ethics operates within a commercial framework that often sits uneasily with the advice being offered. Programs that profile "extreme cheapskates" (Extreme Cheapskates, 2012–), who have chosen to adopt an ethic of thrift, exemplify television's contradictory relationship to alternative consumer ethics. People who forage dumpsters, reuse materials, and impose strict ascetic regimens on themselves and their families are presented as abnormal, extreme and exotic, whatever their reasons. Their tips and advice are not taken seriously, but are offered as voyeuristic and humorous entertainment. The individualized focus of programs that advocate less controversial ethical aims like recycling, eating healthy and locally sourced food, and conserving energy rarely engage with wider societal issues like corporate pollution or environmental policy. Nor do they acknowledge the class and race politics of the ethical regimens they promise—for example, the problem of "food deserts" where nutritional food is neither affordable nor available. As with other programming on lifestyle cable brands, these shows assume that TV viewers have the material resources (education, income, leisure) to take up the advice on offer, and contribute to the idea that politics is a matter of pursuing ethical lifestyle choices, not collective organizing for social change.

Still, the invitation to develop an ethical relationship with oneself can have progressive dimensions that are especially evident in lifestyle and reality programs that aim to rework and diversify gender and sexual identities. Anti-makeover programs like More to Love (2009), True Beauty (2009), The Price of Beauty (2010) and How to Look Good Naked (2008–2010) claim to empower women by problematizing internalized mainstream beauty norms and cultivating body acceptance and self-esteem. On How to Look Good Naked, experts deploy an ethic of care to emotionally bond with participants who believe they are unattractive and unshapely on the outside, and present suggestions,

Figure 2.2 Tiny House Hunters is one of a number of shows that bring the tiny house movement to lifestyle television.

techniques and challenges to encourage the women to re-evaluate their perceptions and improve their ethical relationship with their inner selves. The tone is earnest and sincere, and while the path to self-esteem involves learning to dress and accessorize one's body type (paving the way for "plus-sized" product placements), the message that anyone can be beautiful and attractive if they feel good about themselves does provide an alternative to the narrow beauty ideals and fat shaming perpetuated by many makeovers. But the suggestion that women can overcome feelings of unworthiness and social marginalization, and achieve their goals (romance, careers) in life with a boost of self-esteem, is a dubious one. How to Look Good Naked and similar "make under" programs are complicated interventions that challenge some gender ideologies, but minimize their societal causes and pitch self-work not social change as the solution.

MTV's Girl Code (2010–) combines an ethic of care with humor and irreverence. In what is promoted as a hilarious, over-the-top "how-to manual" for young womanhood, a diverse range of female comics, actresses and athletes offer "rules girls can use for any and every situation" in areas of everyday life ranging from dating and sex to shopping and exercising. These guides to femininity speak from a variety of personal experiences and address the TV viewer as a friend. The ethics and "rules" governing female behavior are not imposed by authorities or experts but are assumed to emerge from a community of women looking out for one another. "There's a sisterhood that women share, and its tenet is simple: We're in this together! Surviving the wonders and woes of the female sex demands that its members abide by the 'code' because, you know, starting a catfight on the dance floor or cutting a bathroom line is not cool," explains the *Girl Code* website. While *Girl Code* can certainly be charged with stereotyping women's love of shopping and investment in heterosexual romance, it does present self-making as a transparent and collective process. The female mentors reflect, in unusually frank (and sometimes contradictory) ways, on topics (including hook-up sex, female orgasm and vaginal health) that are usually considered too taboo for television. By trading experts for ordinary women who speak from personal experience, the show references women's subjugated knowledges, or knowledges that have been "disqualified as inadequate to their task or insufficiently elaborated: naïve knowledges, located low on the hierarchy, below the required level of cognition or scientificity" (Foucault 1980, 82). *Girl Code* does not impose a moral framework on women, much as it encourages TV viewers to learn from women who share intimate reflections about their experiences of sexuality, food, the female body, friendship and everyday life, and circulate suggestions for living based on these histories. In this sense, the program comes closer than self-improvement-oriented lifestyle and reality shows to cultivating the new "aesthetics of existence" implied by Foucault (Gauntlett 2008, 142).

RuPaul's Drag Race (2009–) links the aesthetics of existence to a questioning of gender and sexual norms, and puts fashion and style to alternative uses. In this competition, participants compete to be crowned "America's next drag superstar" as determined by a panel of judges, a quest that involves performing across gender lines. As Joshua Gamson points out, *Drag Race*, like drag culture in general, consistently critiques and complicates the fixity of gender and sexuality. As men are transformed into women, the performative basis of femininity and masculinity is revealed and accentuated, and gender and sexuality identities become more fluid. Host RuPaul, a celebrity drag performer and former model, mentors the contestants, offering advice on the stylization and performance of gender via an ethic of care. Her aim is to help the participants, the drag community and TV viewers overcome the "adversity of gender norms and stigma" through his mantra of Charisma, Uniqueness, Nerve and Talent (Gamson 2014, 242). RuPaul is an intimate expert of subjectivity, who understands the reflexive project of the self as a means to expose and subvert the artificiality of norms. *Drag Race* and spinoffs such as *RuPaul's Drag Race Untucked* (2010–) encourage an inclusive approach to self-fashioning that allows for a diversity of ethics and promotes collective social change. More than other lifestyle experts, RuPaul also celebrates the pleasure of self-making and re-making. As she states in *Workin' It: RuPaul's Guide to Life, Liberty and the Pursuit of Style*, a book billed as a "navigation system through the bumpy road of life," style is a "celebratory celebration of your life force. You must approach it with a sense of joie de vivre. Open yourself to the possibilities!" (2010, xiv).

Recently, a handful of reality programs revolving around the lives of transgender people have provided a cultural platform to explore ethical questions and approaches to self-making rarely featured in mainstream media (*I Am Cait*, 2015– ; *I Am Jazz*, 2015–). In her much-promoted show, newly transgender Caitlyn Jenner of the Kardashian family explores with the help of her famous stepdaughters how to fashion a female self, how to be and act as a woman, and how to live a beautiful life. The program features recurring scenes in which members of the transgender community share their stories, and activists discuss collective self-making ethics and struggles over resources and rights for transgender people. In a number of episodes, Jenner's new friend, national Gay and Lesbian Alliance Against Defamation (GLAAD) co-chair and Barnard College English professor, Jenny Boylan, also a transgender woman, calls her to task for perpetuating gender essentialism and heterosexual norms by expressing a desire for men to treat her as a "normal" woman. Boylan operates as a caring mentor, encouraging Jenner to challenge the definition of normal, and redefine femininity and sexuality in her own terms. She also reminds Jenner that she's part of a community of "sisterhood." While steeped in melodramatic conventions geared to ratings and doubling as a promotion for the Kardashian and Jenner brands, *I Am Cait* nonetheless presents a rare space to negotiate new ethical formations and techniques of self-fashioning with the larger transgender community.

ENTERPRISING SELVES

Lifestyle and reality television circulate multiple aesthetic strategies, forms of expertise and ethical frameworks for fashioning identities and lifestyles. Since the late 1990s, the self as project has increasingly intersected with a self-enterprising logic. This logic is connected to a growing tendency to extend the values of the marketplace into domains that were not previously considered economic, like selfhood and personal relationships. As many critics have argued, societal trends of deregulation, privatization, public-sector downsizing and welfare reform have been accompanied by a shift in the way individuals are encouraged to make themselves into subjects. In neoliberal societies, the marketplace has become the dominant grid for much social life, including self-making and everyday living (Read 2009). Increasingly, we are all called upon to operate as *entrepreneurs of the self* (Rose 1996; Foucault 2010), who embrace values like competition and personal branding, invest in our "human capital" and maximize our quotidian choices to our own strategic advantage. Nikolas Rose argues that enterprising logic draws from and exploits processes of individuation and the care of the self for dispersed political agendas. As we will see in later chapters, self-enterprising subjects are integral to forms of governing at a distance that enlist citizens as the managers of their health, prosperity, security and futures (Rose 1992, 1996).

The logic of enterprise operates across a range of lifestyle and reality programs that apply market concepts (cost–benefit ratios, audits, strategic outcomes, branding) to matters of style, domesticity, relationships, the family and personal life. Life coaches—a new type of expert that originated in the corporate sector—have become more prevalent on these shows; their entrepreneurial, results-oriented strategies for self-transformation circulate in tandem with other modes of guiding individuals. The mantra of *tough love* deployed on many reality programs fuses an ethic of care to the mantra of self-enterprise, and stitches intimate expertise to authoritarian and humiliating strategies rationalized in the name of prompting people to help themselves. One of the most enduring reality formats is the life intervention, in which tough love experts observe, diagnose and transform human subjects while the camera rolls. Since the late 1990s, interventions have proliferated across daytime and primetime, broadcast and cable channels, taking real people as the raw material for addressing a proliferating range of perceived problems, from unemployment and criminality to obesity and divorce. Assisting failing or "at risk" individuals to overcome their situations and improve their relationship with themselves frequently hinges on adopting an enterprising ethic, as exemplified by Dr. Phil (2002–). Hosted by Philip McGraw, Ph.D., a psychologist turned entrepreneur who also has a bestselling line of self-help books and workbooks, Dr. Phil claims to help mainly lower-income women "maximize themselves" and achieve the "results they want" in an increasingly competitive world through personal audits, cost/ratio analyses of behavior, and other technologies of the self adapted from the marketplace (Ouellette and Wilson 2011). "As your life manager," it is your job to "keep you safe and secure from foolish risks, create opportunities for you to get what you really want in this life, take care of your health and well being," McGraw tells his customers. It is up to you to "require more of yourself in your grooming, self-control, emotional management, interaction with others . . . and in every other category you can think of" (McGraw 1999, 169–170).

Dating shows also apply an economic grid to social experience and personal life. In Tough Love (2009–2013), a commercial matchmaker coaches women who have "failed" to find the romantic partners of their dreams. Through weekly lectures, tests, lessons and experiments, the women are taught to evaluate themselves through the eyes of potential male partners conceived as shoppers. As they detach from themselves, they are taught to conceive of themselves as commodities that must be successfully packaged and sold in a competitive dating milieu. At the same time, the participants of the dating boot camp are taught to become managers of themselves who, after coaching from the matchmaker, will make strategic decisions about their makeup, hairstyle, wardrobe, body language, voice, mannerisms and personality geared to maximizing desired outcomes. The neoliberal idea of the self as a repository of human capital, in which individuals must invest to receive returns, takes an explicitly feminized form in Tough Love as the perpetual management of the self intersects with gendered assumptions about the body, beauty, sexuality and social power. While heterosexuality and marriage are enforced as norms, the "problem" addressed by the life intervention (being unmarried) is presented as a failure of feminine self-enterprise, and solved accordingly.

An ethic of self-enterprise also underscores a growing number of makeover and style programs. The conception of the self as never-ending reflexive project is compatible with a market-oriented approach to everyday life, as exemplified by *Real Housewives* cast member and lifestyle entrepreneur Bethany Frankel's mantra for losing weight and staying slim: "It's all about checks and balances. Your diet is a bank account." Across lifestyle brands like the Food Network and HGTV, cooking and home programming has been infused with market sensibilities and the demonstration of self-enterprise. How-to cooking shows are overshadowed by high-stakes competitions like *MasterChef* (2010–), *Top Chef* (2006–), *Hell's Kitchen* (2005–), *Iron Chef America* (2005–) and *Cupcake Wars* (2009–2013). Home improvement programs increasingly approach home ownership as a moneymaking enterprise as much as (or more than) a consumer choice. Programs like *Curb Appeal* (1999–2011) and *Property Brothers* (2011–) apply an economic lens to the family home, and encourage and facilitate "quotidian" forms of financialization through domestic real estate (Allon 2010; Hay 2010). Programs about flipping houses for profit—often after the former owners have been forcibly evicted due to financial hardships—have become nearly as pervasive as decorating, fixer-upper and real estate shows in recent years. *Flip this House* (2005–2009), *Flip It to Win It* (2013–), *Flip or Flop* (2013–) and similar shows construct the foreclosed home as a business opportunity to be seized by enterprising individuals. The housing crisis triggered by the financial crisis and the recession that followed, and the trauma of dispossession engendered by soaring home foreclosure rates, are glossed over as other people's problems. An ethic of bare enterprise underscores the frenzy of financial speculation, risk assessments and fierce competition that unfolds as self-interested entrepreneurs scramble to bid on foreclosed properties they are not allowed to inspect in advance, and carry out quick and cheap renovations in the hopes of maximizing the return on their investment.

Reality programs revolving around pawn shops, auto repossession agencies and storage locker auctions take the logic of self-enterprise to its final conclusion. In these shows, which proliferated in the wake of the recession, the chronic poverty and misfortune of the lower classes is narrated as an entrepreneurial goldmine. Week after week, this strand of programming enacts an everyday version of the global process that David

Figure 2.3 The contents of storage lockers up for auction on *Storage Wars* are reduced to dollar amounts.

Harvey calls "accumulation by dispossession" (2004), as small business owners and entrepreneurs capitalize on the seizure of personal property (furnishings, automobiles, electronics, heirlooms) in the course of everyday economic practices. Hyper-competitive, calculating and willing to rationalize the hardship of others in brazenly self-interested terms, the mostly male characters perform an extreme version of *homo economicus*, the self-enterprising subjectivity traced by Michel Foucault in his genealogy of neoliberalism in the West (2010). Ruthlessly, they reduce seized consumer goods, and other investments in individuation, identity and the "good life," to dollar amounts and profit ratios. Those who lack or lose property are stripped of individualism altogether, registering only anonymous and disposable populations, integral to the business of recessionary profiteering, but relegated to the periphery of a society imagined in free market terms. While this hardcore enactment of self-enterprise is especially shocking and cruel, it arguably only magnifies elements of a self-interested market sensibility operating across a growing spectrum of lifestyle and reality television.

3

GOVERNING CITIZENS

In 2012, Michelle Obama appeared on The Biggest Loser (2004–), a reality competition in which people compete to lose the most weight for a $250,000 prize. In a special two-part episode, cast members receive makeovers before traveling to Washington, DC, to visit the White House and meet the First Lady, who joins them for a rigorous session of jumping jacks and squats in the East Room. Dubbing the event the "first ever White House workout," Obama used her appearance on the long-running TV show to promote Let's Move, an initiative she developed to help "solve the problem of obesity" in America by encouraging citizens to make healthier lifestyle choices, such as exercising regularly and eating fruits and vegetables with every meal. Aiming to "get results within a generation," Let's Move is especially concerned to help children avoid obesity. This involves teaching adults how their behavior impacts young people, and offering advice and resources for change, among other strategies. Connecting The Biggest Loser to Let's Move's mission to improve the health of the nation, Obama told the contestants: "You are all showing millions of Americans that each of us can make positive changes in our lives and these changes won't just make a difference for ourselves, they can make an impact on our families and children as well."

Let's Move is affiliated with the Partnership for a Healthier America (PHA), a nonprofit organization that works with the private sector to "ensure the health of our nation's youth by solving the childhood obesity crisis."

With Michelle Obama as honorary chair and dozens of corporate partners including insurance companies, hospitals, retailers (Kwik Trip, Walmart) and consumer brands (Birds Eye, Dannon, Del Monte, Nike, Reebok), the organization aims to "make the healthy choice the easy choice for kids and families." To get kids and their parents moving more and eating better, PHA spearheads efforts to infuse popular media culture with educational messages. For example, the organization worked with hip hop artists to create *Songs for a Healthier America*, an album that "matches health-minded lyrics with pop beats" in the hopes of getting kids "excited about living healthfully." In 2013, PHA teamed up with Obama and partners "across the public and private sectors," including Aquafina, Nestlé Pure Life, Poland Spring, Dasani, Evian, Ice Mountain and other bottled water brands, to "encourage people to drink water more often." In another TV appearance sponsored by the Brita water-filtration brand, the First Lady returned to *The Biggest Loser* to explain the health benefits of proper hydration and encourage TV viewers to "drink up."

The partnership between *The Biggest Loser*, the White House, nonprofit organizations and corporate sponsors mobilizes lifestyle and reality television for the purpose of making and guiding citizens. At first glance, the surge of popular lifestyle and reality entertainment focused on self-making and lifestyle may seem like a retreat from democracy and civic culture (Taylor 2002). Typically, only nonfiction formats that inform TV viewers about public issues (documentaries, "serious" journalism, televised political debates) are understood as resources for citizenship. With the deregulation of broadcasting and the waning of public interest mandates, television is no longer required to present these civic resources, which are far less profitable than entertainment and newer forms of infotainment and reality entertainment. Public broadcasting, which was created in the 1960s to provide more robust news and informational programming regardless of ratings or profit ratios, has also been transformed by market forces (Ouellette 2009). The perception that civic-oriented information and documentary has been replaced by more lucrative species of lifestyle instruction and factual entertainment has worried critics (Corner 2002). One issue of concern is that television no longer supports—and perhaps even undermines—the democratic ideal of self-government, which requires informed citizens who actively participate in public affairs. While these concerns are valid, it is too simplistic to assume that television has turned its back on citizenship altogether. If we look more closely at lifestyle and reality entertainment, we can see that television has helped create a new model of citizenship that puts more emphasis on private institutions, individual choice and self-empowerment than before.

This path to good citizenship is more apt to be paved with consumer choices, lifestyle experts and brands—topics addressed in earlier chapters—than with courthouses, elections or town halls, although these formal markers of government are incorporated into the conventions of lifestyle and reality entertainment in programs ranging from *Style by Jury* (2015–) to *American Idol* (2002–2015). Sometimes, lifestyle and reality programming is directly aligned with the institutions of official government, as with Obama's role on *The Biggest Loser*. Usually, television's involvement in shaping and guiding citizens is more informal and dispersed. Many popular lifestyle and reality programs align with strategies of governing rooted in neoliberal rationalities of privatization, personal responsibility and self-enterprise, without making any reference to public authorities. The impetus to solve problems (such as obesity), and assist needy and "at risk" individuals through lifestyle and reality entertainment is also connected to a rising ethic of corporate social responsibility (CSR) among television networks

Figure 3.1 First Lady Michelle Obama exercises with contestants on *The Biggest Loser* at the White House.

and sponsors. Unlike broadcast regulations enforced by the State, CSR is a voluntary practice that is often connected to creating brand value. While Obama's visit lent credibility to *The Biggest Loser*'s mission, the show was thriving as an informal technology of citizenship long before her arrival.

While *The Biggest Loser* generates enormous profit for NBC and advertisers (Jello, Subway, Planet Fitness, Jennie-O, General Mills) whose brands are integrated into the competition, it is also billed as a gesture of corporate goodwill—an attempt by the TV industry and the corporate sector to help solve the "obesity epidemic." TV viewers are encouraged to use the program as motivation and empower themselves through the online *Biggest Loser* boot camp, a website with tips on diet and exercise, and *Biggest Loser* self-help books, cookbooks and fitness DVDs. Even if most TV viewers don't make any changes in their lives, the program perpetuates the idea that citizens must take responsibility for their health, and that commercial television supports this goal. In this sense, the show does not entirely abandon the (no longer enforced) concept of serving the public interest, as much as it reinvents television's contribution to democracy and self-government in profitable, privatized and personalized terms.

This chapter introduces lifestyle and reality television as a cultural technology of *citizenship*. I discuss television's relationship to theories of governmentality, or dispersed efforts to shape and guide the conduct of individuals and populations "at a distance," and situate the privatized and personalized templates for citizenship it enacts within a context of neoliberal policies, discourses and reforms. I discuss how a range of programs, in partnership with commercial sponsors and (sometimes) non-profit agencies, steer self-governing individuals toward the desired outcomes of experts and authorities, and point to some contradictions in this process.

TELEVISION, GOVERNMENTALITY AND THE NEOLIBERAL PROJECT

Because so much lifestyle and reality programming circulates information, advice and templates for self-shaping and better living, it is especially compatible with neoliberal strategies of "governing at a distance" that gained currency as public welfare programs were downsized in the 1990s. The "reinvention of government" during this decade involved reducing and outsourcing many publicly funded social services, and creating strategic partnerships between public agencies, nonprofits and corporations (Ouellette and Hay 2008). Citizens were in turn addressed as the agents of their destinies, who achieved goals of health, happiness, productivity, security and well being through their individual choices and self-care practices. This message, which permeated policy and political discourse, coincided with the intensification of forms of cultural training that govern indirectly in the name of lifestyle maximization, individual choice and personal responsibility. Theorists refer to this dispersed process of guiding and shaping citizens as *governmentality*.

The term governmentality refers to the processes through which individuals shape and guide their own conduct—and that of others—with particular aims and objectives in mind (Foucault 1991; Gordon 1991; Burchell 1996). This informal process is distinguished from (though complementary to) the rule of law from institutions and practices of official government (such as voting). Scholars of governmentality emphasize the proliferation and diffusion of everyday techniques through which individuals and populations are expected to reflect upon, work on and regulate themselves as an implicit condition of their citizenship. These techniques do not emanate directly from the State, nor can they be traced to any singular power center. Techniques of governmentality are circulated in a dispersed fashion by a range of experts and intermediaries, and the institutions (schools, social work, medicine) that authorize their knowledge and expertise. Television, along with other popular media, are an important—if much less examined—part of this mix (Ouellette and Hay 2008) in that they too have operated as technologies called upon to guide and shape citizens "who do not need to be governed by others, but will govern themselves, master themselves, care for themselves" (Rose 1996, 45).

Nikolas Rose argues that the "regulation of conduct" in late modern capitalist societies is rarely associated with a top-down agenda, but is more often presented as the individual's "own desire" to achieve optimum happiness and success (Rose 1996, 57–59). While, in earlier periods of industrial capitalism, social workers and other experts were enlisted to monitor and police the everyday behavior of immigrants and the working classes, today mechanisms of social control work differently. "Social work, as a means of civilization under tutelage, gives way to the private counselor, the self-help manual and the telephone helpline, as practices whereby each individual binds themselves to expert advice as a matter of their own freedom," Rose contends. The regulation of conduct then "becomes a matter of each individual's desire to govern their own conduct freely in the service of the maximization of a version of their happiness and fulfillment that they take to be their own, but such lifestyle maximization entails a relation to authority in the very moment as it pronounces itself the outcome of free choice" (Rose 1996, 58–59). While harsher means of governing are still widely deployed to govern marginalized populations deemed unruly or unable to govern themselves, more dispersed forms of governmentality, often operating through media and consumer culture, assist "good citizens" to regulate their own conduct in the name of personal choice, freedom and self-empowerment.

Governmentality relies on *technologies of the self*, a concept discussed in earlier chapters. Michel Foucault defined technologies of the self as "procedures, which no doubt exist in every civilization, suggested or prescribed to individuals in order to determine their identity, maintain it, or transform it in terms of a certain number of ends, through relations of self-mastery and self-knowledge" (1997, 87). Governmentality, he argued, is the "contact point" where the dispersed agendas of institutions, experts and authorities meet the process by which "the individual acts on himself," and technologies of the self are "integrated into the structures of coercion" (Burchell 1996, 20). This approach to democracy seeks to understand how freedom and governing work together, and how citizens are trained to meet the expectations that are placed on them. Scholars of governmentality cite media as a cultural technology that, operating outside "public powers," works to govern the "capacities, competencies and wills of subjects," and in so doing, translate the "goals of authorities into choices and commitments of individuals" (Rose 1996, 58). Lifestyle and reality television has been stitched into contemporary dynamics of governmentality, helping to translate neoliberal policies and discourses as opportunities for individuals to empower themselves through their conduct and choices (Ouellette and Hay 2008).

Developments like entertainment-education and social marketing are especially suitable to strategies of governing at a distance. The "edutainment" tradition seeks to weave the social education goals of official governments and nonprofit organizations into forms of popular entertainment (such as soap operas). Established by social scientists as a way to promote birth control, healthy water consumption, and other health and population goals in the developing world, edutainment uses the pleasure associated with entertainment to lure audiences to educational messages designed to shape and guide everyday conduct. Social marketing campaigns, which have proliferated recently in the United States and other Western capitalist democracies, attempt to reform individuals in specific and measurable ways, such as getting them to quit smoking (O'Reagan, Balnaves and Sternberg 2002). Usually organized as collaborations between the commercial sector and nonprofit agencies, social marketing campaigns apply the techniques of advertising and promotion to reach targeted populations in the hopes of intervening in their attitudes and behavior. The hope is that viewers will "diffuse, multiply and facilitate the take up of the behavioral norms and values being promoted" of their own accord, a goal that is assumed to be particularly effective in contexts where objectives are transparent, and audiences are invited to become "co-creators" of governmental objectives (2002, 19). In the United States, social marketing techniques have been integrated into lifestyle and reality entertainment promoting weight loss, recycling, delayed parenting and other objectives.

James Hay and I have argued that lifestyle and reality television aligns especially well with neoliberal understandings of citizenship that problematize "dependency" on State resources. This is especially evident in programs that seek to solve widespread societal problems like unemployment and criminality by transforming so-called needy or "at risk" individuals into responsible and self-enterprising citizens. While prosperous lifestyle and consumer clusters are offered a plethora of advice for maximizing their health, security, finances and happiness by a growing number of cable lifestyle channels, the audience for this programming is conceived as already capable of handling the demands of citizenship. Hybrid reality formats, including the makeover and the life intervention, problematize the conduct, choices, bodies and lifestyles of disadvantaged and subordinated "other" people, inviting the TV audience to revel in its own normalcy while also learning lessons about good citizenship indirectly via the cautionary tales presented on screen. These programs disproportionately cast women, working- and lower-class individuals and people of color as under-maximized individuals who can be helped by experts to empower themselves.

One of the goals that lifestyle and reality television has consistently taken up is self-sufficiency. In the US, daytime programs like *Judge Judy* (1999–) and *Dr. Phil* (2002–) began to problematize "welfare dependency" in tandem with the passage of the Personal Responsibility Act of 1996, which placed strict limits and restrictions on public assistance programs. Across cable and broadcast channels, many other programs have encouraged real people, often marginalized by gender, race and class, to take charge of their own fates and fortunes without making demands on society, thereby reproducing the mantra of self-sufficiency less directly. For example, makeover shows often connect the transformation of the "outer body" to the actualization of inner capacities for success in a precarious workforce (Ouellette and Hay 2008; Weber 2009; Sender 2012). In the United Kingdom, television's relationship to welfare reform is more overt, due in part to national differences. While the US has historically provided minimal State assistance to citizens in need, the UK and many other European nations developed a collective approach to public welfare that encompassed free health care and more robust financial benefits for the poor and unemployed. As neoliberal discourses and policies have taken hold globally, this collective model has been challenged and reformed, and citizens have been recast as entrepreneurs of the self who must take responsibility for their own welfare.

A number of reality series have facilitated this responsibilization process. *Benefit Busters* (2009) chronicles the British government's attempts to "revolutionize the welfare system by rewarding private companies according to their ability to coax people off benefits and into jobs." The first episode follows a mandatory adult education course led by a private employment coach that aims to give single parents on benefits the "skills and confidence to enter the workplace and convince them that they'll be better off doing so." *The Fairy Job Mother* (2010) follows Hayley Taylor, the employment coach from *Benefit Busters*, as she continues to advise people who have relied on government assistance in order to help them find jobs. In episodes designed for emotional drama, she "moves in with a family of long-term benefit claimants, observes the habits of the household, and produces a plan of action" (Aitkenhead 2010). As Hannah Hamad points out, Taylor promotes the idea that any barriers to employment can be "surmounted by individual willpower" regardless of any social inequities or power balances in play (2014, 225), and has modeled the mantra of self-enterprise associated with neoliberalism by parlaying her television exposure into celebrity status and a thriving brand of expertise. Benefits Street (2010), a controversial documentary series that took TV viewers inside the lives of low-income benefits recipients whom many critics felt were pathologized for ratings, generated the spinoff There's Help Out There (2015). Exemplifying the move from dependency to self-enterprise, one of the former residents of "Benefits Street" coaches other people "living on state welfare to wean themselves off benefits" like she did. In 2015, the British Broadcasting Company (BBC), one of the world's oldest and largest public broadcasters, announced plans for a reality show called Britain's Hardest Grafter, which pits chronically unemployed and low-paid workers against one another for a cash prize. According to the publicity, the purpose of this Hunger Games-type experiment is to test poor people's work ethic: contestants will be given various jobs over the course of the season and the "least effective" workers will be ousted. Meanwhile, a crop of new shows like My Great Big Benefits Wedding (2015–), 12 Years Old and on Benefits (2015–), Benefits and Bypasses: Billion Pound Bypasses (2015–) and Undercover Benefits Cheat (2015–) incorporate the benefit-busting theme into reality entertainment geared to ratings.

In the United States, federal welfare reform initiatives peaked in the late 1990s with the Personal Responsibility Act. However, the financial crisis of 2008 and the economic recession it triggered led to soaring unemployment rates, home foreclosures and financial distress for a growing number of people, who often needed help with things like food and housing. Within this context, a cluster of reality programs emerged to document and assist individuals and families impacted by a recessionary economy. Shows like Downsized (2010) chronicled the trials of an affluent white family that lost their large suburban home when the father's company collapsed, highlighting their cost-cutting strategies (like making their own gourmet coffee drinks) and enterprising efforts to keep the family afloat through various home businesses. On these shows, public forms of assistance, such as unemployment benefits and the Supplemental Nutrition Assistance Program (formerly food stamps), were not mentioned, let alone utilized. Contrary to the self-sufficient and enterprising family depicted on *Downsized*, the U.S. version of *The Fairy Job Mother* (2010) intervened in the lives of "severely job-challenged" families who were not bouncing back from chronic unemployment. Featuring the employment coach from the British series, the debut episode set the tone by featuring a low-income white family that had been relying on military benefits set to expire. Both parents are young and unemployed. Without college degrees or vocational training, they are qualified only for minimum-wage jobs that barely cover the expense of day care for their two toddlers. When Taylor arrives at their modest apartment, she discovers a sink full of dirty dishes, unfolded laundry strewn about and dog feces on the floor—props that evoke stereotypical assumptions about the laziness and faulty self-care practices of the poor. She subjects the young couple to severe scrutiny and surveillance, lecturing them about their spending habits, counseling them on personal grooming and self-esteem, and setting up hidden cameras to record their encounters with potential employers. While the show's opening credits acknowledge a rising "crisis" of unemployment in the United States, the solution to this urgent problem is individualized and privatized. In this sense, *The Fairy Job Mother*, like many TV interventions, aligns governmentality with a neoliberal model of citizenship (Ouellette 2014a).

Reality programs that claim to address and resolve the problem of criminality also downplay collective responsibilities and societal causes. In recent years, the U.S. television industry has partnered with a dizzying number of law enforcement agencies, police forces, specialized crime units and prisons to produce reality shows that often claim to help deter and manage crime, in addition to entertaining audiences for profit. Sometimes, these programs adapt the technologies of the self that circulate on makeover and intervention programs for "potential" or convicted criminals. Low-income men of color are particularly targeted for expert guidance and transformation, perpetuating the racialization of criminality without addressing racial and class inequalities or policing methods that profile populations deemed unruly and risky. On T.I.'s *Road to Redemption* (2009), the rap star operates as an ordinary expert who attempts to discourage criminal behavior among young male Latino and African Americans. The show arose from a bargain that T.I. struck with an Atlanta Superior Court Judge following his arrest for weapons charges. In exchange for a reduced sentence, he was placed under house arrest and subjected to electronic monitoring. T.I. was also required to perform 1,000 hours of community service in which he was to discourage "at risk" youth from following in his footsteps. This sentencing requirement was woven in to the advertising-sponsored MTV series, which also provided a platform for bolstering T.I.'s musical career. In episodes like "You Are Responsible for Your Own Actions" and "Own Your Mistake," T.I. is shown speaking to school and community groups about personal responsibility. He also works with teenagers such as Peewee, a "hustler" from New Jersey who is African American. As part of his "redemption," T.I. asks Peewee to spend hours in a jail cell and takes him on a field trip to the city morgue in order to "learn about the consequences of crime" and develop better "decision-making" skills.

Figure 3.2 A contestant on *From G's to Gents* listens to an expert discuss dining etiquette and wine.

Often, the governmentality enacted on lifestyle and reality television is contradictory. Tensions can arise between the goals of entertaining and problem solving, maximizing profit and staging corporate social responsibility. Such is the case with From G's to Gents (2008–2009), a makeover competition in which former P. Diddy assistant and hip hop stylist Fonzworth Bentley, author of Advance Your Swagger: How to Use Manners, Confidence, and Style to Get Ahead (2007), sets out to transform so-called gangsters, some of whom are homeless and have spent time in jail, into respectable gentlemen. With a team of experts (including Ted Allen, the food and wine specialist from Queer Eye for the Straight Guy, and other TV personalities) he teaches contestants sequestered in a mansion how to eat, dress and speak "properly" as they compete for a place in Bentley's Gentleman's Club. Each week, the least gentlemanly contestant (as determined by Bentley) is asked to remove his blue blazer with the club's insignia and is sent home; the final contestant wins the game and is awarded a cash prize. While From G's to Gents is steeped in entertainment conventions and has a playful sensibility, it is serious about reducing criminality by transforming starkly disadvantaged young men into respectable members of society. Moreover, the show presents itself as a life-saving intervention in the lives of the participants themselves. Early in the first episode, a contestant articulates the stakes of the competition, telling the camera "I'm either dead or in jail if I don't change" (Page 2015, 439).

This remark, argues Allison Page, "indexes the ways the criminalization of blackness combined with poverty" reduces the young man's "options to death or incarceration." Many of the contestants are similarly criminalized, but From G's to Gents claims to provide them with a "third option." To help the men change their destinies, Fonzworth draws on his rags-to-riches narrative as a self-made hip hop celebrity, as well as an "exaggerated etiquette harkening back to a particularly aristocratic, white, leisure class lifestyle" that plays for laughs to the extent that the contestants are unable to distinguish among fine wines or master sports like cricket (2015, 440). The program conceals the inequalities of a supposedly postracial society marked by the demise of affirmative action policies and programs and the expansion of mass incarceration, but as a platform for governmentality it is ultimately contradictory, says Page. While From G's to Gents enacts a neoliberal logic of self-enterprising citizenship by staging personal responsibilization as a competition with an economic reward, it fails to transform the contestants who, lacking the advantages and resources of the white middle class, are unable to govern themselves and "manage their freedom" in the proscribed ways. At the same time, she notes, some contestants resist and exploit the logic of the show by rejecting white middle-class expertise, admitting to being in the game only for the prize, and performing a stylized black masculinity evocative of the black dandy, a figure that has historically disrupted racial, class and sexual norms. Even as shows like *From G's to Gents* enact self-enterprising templates for citizenship, they may point to widening contradictions and points of resistance within neoliberal discourse.

THE BIOPOLITICS OF HEALTH

Health is another issue that connects lifestyle and reality television to dispersed forms of citizenship training and governing at a distance. The liberal State has long been invested in shaping the health of the citizenry—a process that scholars call *biopolitics*. This term refers to technologies of power that "manage and control the life of the population" (Nadesan 2010, 2). Biopolitics operates through disciplines (statistics, demography and biology) that "make it possible to analyze life processes on the level of populations" and to govern on the basis of such knowledge (Lemke 2011, 5). This involves identifying, representing and managing risks to the "optimization" of the population and particular subsets of it, such as children or young women (Nadesan 2010, 2), through coercive mechanisms, therapeutic programs or self-help initiatives. Obama's Let's Move campaign is biopolitical in that it draws from scientific research that deems obesity risky and mobilizes citizens to maximize their health. While public agencies, universities and scientific research centers have always been instrumental to biopolitics, today market forces play a more visible role and health is increasingly governed at a distance. "Healthy bodies and hygienic homes may still be a public value and a political objective. But we no longer need state bureaucracies to enjoin healthy habits of eating, of personal hygiene, of tooth care and the like, with compulsory inspection, subsidized incentives to eat or drink correctly, and so forth," writes Rose. "In the new domain of consumption, individuals will want to be healthy, experts will instruct them on how to be so, and entrepreneurs will exploit and enhance this market for health. Health will be ensured through a combination of the market, expertise and a regulated autonomy (Rose 1998, 155).

As Sarah Nettleton argues, the "optimization" of health has come to involve the "consumption of a range of goods and services which are increasingly marketed for their health-giving properties." In sync with neoliberal rationalities of governing, health has become personalized, as citizens are called upon to exercise their right—and duty—to "maintain, contribute to and ensure their health status." As with other aspects of welfare, health is orchestrated not through the State but through dispersed networks of government encompassing public agencies, insurance companies, nonprofit organizations and corporations. Citizens are also expected to monitor a "wide range of risks," as determined by experts, and to "calculate likely consequences of certain actions for themselves" (1997, 208). Health management under neoliberalism calls on citizens to manage their body weight, stress and levels of exercise as care of the self. As Majia Nadesan point out, consumers are now offered a dizzying array of products and techniques for "maximizing health, from organic products and vitamins to fitness training." As health becomes integrated into the fashioning of the self, "affluent populations often flaunt their wellness as a form of social currency" (2008, 111).

The proliferation of lifestyle and reality programming aimed at health-conscious consumer clusters is part of this trend. On daytime television, programs like The Doctors (2008–) and Dr. Oz (2009–) circulate consumer-oriented health advice in an "easily digestible, down-to-earth manner" (both programs also operate informational websites and Dr. Oz has a spinoff magazine). The Discovery Health cable network is entirely devoted to health programming, from advice programs to reality shows set in hospitals and clinics to Mystery Diagnosis (2005–2011), a constantly rerun stalwart that claims to help consumers whose "bizarre symptoms" have been misdiagnosed or are baffling their doctors. Addressing the TV viewer as the active manager of his or her health, this programming perpetuates the optimization of health through consumption, individual choice and the mastery of self-care. Yet, the transformation of passive patients into self-enterprising and empowered consumers can also undermine and disrupt the authority of the medical establishment. TV personality Dr. Mahmet Oz has been criticized for enabling this disruption by introducing alternative and nontraditional approaches to the expanding array of knowledge, products and services now available for optimizing one's health, because some medical authorities equate these approaches with quackery.

As Nettleton points out, the flip side of the empowered health consumer is the individual who fails to manage "risk factors which are within the control of the individual." The proper management and care of one's health has become a marker of the "active citizen, the self who can be, and indeed ought to be, in control of his or her self." Likewise, the failure to achieve health may "impact one's social identity in that one is not well, not ill but 'at risk'" (1997, 214). This assumption underscores reality programs that claim to help solve the obesity "epidemic" while entertaining audiences and generating profits. As Lauren Berlant points out, obesity is a good example of how health is increasingly governed through neoliberal biopolitics: networks of insurance companies, public agencies and commercial enterprises produce and circulate knowledge about the problem, identify and govern risks, and mobilize "at risk" individuals to take charge of their health through consumption and self-care (2011, 112–113). Television has been stitched in to this biopolitical process through high-profile interventions like The Biggest Loser and other variations on the weight loss format.

The aims and tactics deployed by weight loss shows vary. On Jamie Oliver's Food Revolution (2010), celebrity chef Jamie Oliver embarks on a journey across the US to reduce obesity by equipping families and children with the "skills they need to lead healthier, happier lives." Besides teaching kids how to optimize their own health, he uses his show to lobby for healthier school lunches and compulsory food education in schools, and in that way connects television—and his celebrity brand—to both the government of the self and societal reforms. Many programs follow the model of The Biggest Loser by staging weight loss as a process of self-transformation that complements and personalizes dispersed efforts to govern the health of citizens, from Let's Move to health-conscious services and brands to corporate wellness programs. Many of these programs are steeped in the competitive values of the marketplace. Billed as a "positive solution-rich reality program" by the Lifetime cable network, Mission Makeover (2009–) promises to help solve the "national epidemic of childhood obesity" by staging a total "health and wellness" makeover competition for women and their families. Experts in nutrition, fitness and lifestyle coach the contestants on weight loss while explicitly feminizing the weight loss competition by linking health to "beauty, self-confidence and style." While all women—and TV viewers at home—are encouraged to take responsibility for their health, only the most enterprising contestant will be crowned the winner and receive the cash prize.

Other programs incorporate weight loss into the docusoap format. *Ruby* (2008–2011) followed an ordinary woman who weighed 500 pounds over several years as she struggled to lose weight. *One Big Happy Family* (2009) chronicles a family in which everyone weighs more than 300 pounds as they attempt to shed pounds, while *Heavy* (2011) follows people with "life threatening health issues because of their obesity" and chronicles their struggle to conquer "food addiction" in an intensive treatment program.

My 600-lb Life (2012–) takes TV viewers inside the everyday lives of "morbidly obese" people who are attempting to qualify for weight loss surgery. As with many docusoaps, the participants are cast as unable to control their appetites and properly govern their food consumption. Cameras follow them as they attempt to shed pounds through exercise and diet regimens supervised by experts. Voyeurism is rampant: on *My 600-lb Life*, cameras routinely follow the subjects into the shower or bath to capture graphic footage of rolls of naked flesh, bed sores and sagging skin as they struggle to wash and use the toilet. This footage signals the "authenticity" of the reality program and functions as evidence of illness, not unlike the "money shot" used to signal the realness of filmed pornographic acts. To varying degrees, other weight loss programs similarly characterize obesity as a disease of the will. As with *The Biggest Loser*, participants are cast as "their own worst enemies, as lazy, passive, self-hating and controlled by excessive appetites" (Sender 2012, 37).

Obesity on television is disproportionately presented as a problem of the working and lower middle classes, but is attributed to their presumed underdeveloped capacities for self-mastery and self-care, not to social inequalities. As Lauren Berlant argues, the "slow death" of the poor and the working classes under neoliberalism, by which she means the "wearing out" of a large segment of the population that is overworked and financially insecure, is obscured by the "crisis management of obesity" led by insurance companies, public health agencies and corporate PR departments (2011, 101–102). Berlant argues that obesity is a social phenomenon, not an individual failure of health management. The declining health or slow death of the disenfranchised working classes can be traced to the waning of the social welfare contract and the widening gap between haves and have-nots who may work multiple low-paid service jobs to make ends meet, lack access to the health-conscious products and services offered to more prosperous consumers, and must rely on cheap processed food. It is this segment of the population that embodies the rising risk of obesity. "Fat characterizes the bodily propensities of working class and subproletarian Americans of all races and regions, especially people of color," while at the same time, the "numbers of poor Americans reporting going without meals, requiring emergency food assistance, or experiencing fairly constant hunger has also increased dramatically since the shrinkage of food programs for the poor in the 1990s," Berlant explains. Tellingly, the vast majority of the "morbidly or very obese are also close to or beneath the poverty line" (2011, 113).

When people who are shamed, lectured and "exhorted" to diet and exercise resist efforts to reform their behavior, they can be exercising a type of resistance, says Berlant. At a time when food is one of the "few spaces of controllable, reliable pleasure" that many poor and working-class people have, refusing to give up this pleasure is not a disease of the will, but a "fitting response to a stressful environment," Berlant argues (2011, 114–115). Weight loss television programs fail to recognize the intersectionality of class, race and obesity, perpetuating the idea that the "crisis" can be managed through a combination of risk management and personal initiative. Yet, while shows like The Biggest Loser and My 600-lb Life participate in neoliberal strategies of governing health, they operate in tension with other logics that equate self-empowerment with fat acceptance. The rise of an identity politics around size, and the expansion of the consumer market for "plus-size" goods, exists in perpetual tension with the construction of obesity as a medical problem and a failure of citizenship. Shows like Big Sexy (2011), a series about fashion bloggers, and More to Love (2009), a dating competition in which "plus-sized" female contestants compete for the attention of a "plus-sized" male suitor, encourage a sense of pride and belonging around size difference. On *My Big Fat Fabulous Life* (2015), a woman who gained notoriety when her video "Fat Girl Dancing" went viral on YouTube, rejects the passive and abnormal subjectivity assigned to fat people. She has pursued a different path to self-enterprising citizenship by launching the #nobodyshamecampaign to promote self-love and acceptance, and harnessing her size to establish herself as a celebrity and personal brand. While neoliberal governmentality often works through lifestyle, it is only one of the logics at work in the lifestyling of television.[1]

REALITY TV AS BIRTH CONTROL

Teenage pregnancy is another issue that reality television approaches as a technology of citizenship and a platform for governing at a distance.[2] The "problem" of teenage pregnancy is of particular concern to neoliberal societies because having a child too early is assumed to undermine the mother's economic self-sufficiency and increase dependency on the State. In recent years, the TV industry has launched a number of reality programs in partnership with private and public agencies that problematize and claim to deter early childbearing (Ouellette 2014b). *The Baby Borrowers* (2008) was billed as a primetime social experiment that takes young people on a "rollercoaster ride of adult responsibility, allowing them to experience parenting first-hand." Promoted with the tagline "It's Not TV, It's Birth Control," the show placed teenage couples in a suburban home, and gave them jobs and babies to manage 24/7 while cameras rolled. A racially diverse cast is put to the test in episodes built around the challenges of assembling cribs, caring for fussy infants (whose parents watch via surveillance cameras), and juggling work and childcare, while the camera lingers on shots of Pampers and other sponsoring brands. Presented as a gesture of corporate social responsibility in partnership with the National Campaign to Prevent Teen and Unplanned Pregnancy, a nonprofit agency, *The Baby Borrowers* mobilizes reality entertainment to align the sexual behaviors and reproductive choices of young people with biopolitical efforts to manage and control early childbearing.

Dad Camp (2010) provides "boot-camp style" therapy to the boyfriends of young unwed pregnant women, in order to help them learn "the responsibility of fatherhood." Created as a partnership with the National Fatherhood Initiative, the show incorporates footage from a speech in which Barack Obama promotes responsible fatherhood into its opening credits. The speech is the basis for enrolling six pregnant couples in their late teens and early twenties in a "boot camp" where the young men sleep on cots in a bunker filled with baby books and undergo intensive treatment to learn adult responsibility. The soon-to-be fathers are cast as low-income, often Latino and African American men, who are addicted to recreational drugs and unwilling to give up a lifestyle based on gambling, loafing and partying. They are characterized as "at risk" for failed citizenship, and as posing a risk to the self-maximization and well being of their female partners. This setup provides the rationale for harsher techniques of normalization, surveillance and therapeutics than we see in *The Baby Borrowers*.

16 and Pregnant (2009–) follows female high school students through the experience of teenage pregnancy and childbirth as a "public education partnership" between MTV and the National Campaign to Prevent Teen and Unplanned Pregnancy. The spinoff, *Teen Mom* (2009–), is a docusoap that follows graduates of 16 and Pregnant and promotes a similar mission of deterring early childbearing. Both productions have spawned multiple seasons and sequels (*Teen Mom 2*, 2011– ; *Teen Mom 3*, 2013–) with new casts, and some of the young mothers have become tabloid celebrities. Combining the conventions of observational documentary and soap opera, and adding sound-bite confessionals and edgy graphics to the mix, both shows generate high ratings (and enormous profits), even as they are also framed as a form of birth control through tie-in social marketing campaigns, after-shows in which the characters are advised by celebrity therapist and TV personality Dr. Drew Pinsky, and the dissemination of study guides and websites emphasizing their purpose as "teachable moments" and "cautionary tales."

However well intended, the enlistment of reality TV entertainment as a mode of family planning needs to be critically analyzed as part of the strategies of governing examined thus far. Teenage pregnancy has long been posited as an "epidemic" closely linked to welfare dependency. Since the 1990s, the issue has been explicitly tied to self-empowerment discourses. When the 1996 Personal Responsibility Act ended welfare as an "entitlement" in the name of empowering citizens to help themselves, a central component of

Figure 3.3 The cast of Teen Mom receives counseling from Dr. Drew Pinsky on the after-show.

the legislation involved helping "young people make responsible choices and delay parenting until they are financially and emotionally ready," in the words of then president Bill Clinton (1997). This objective was linked to the expectation that everyone—whether male, female, young, old, white, or of color—be the self-enterprising managers of their choices and life trajectories. In a move that "posted" inequalities of race, gender and class, the pregnant teenager was characterized as someone who had failed to plan her life appropriately—including preparing for employment—and could no longer depend on the State for assistance. Rising expectations for girls and young women to be financially self-sufficient were joined to the assumption—codified by federal welfare reform legislation—that too-early childbearing undermined their potential. This assumption was made more urgent in light of Centers for Disease Control and Prevention reports indicating that the US has a higher teenage pregnancy rate than any other developed country.

The equation of delayed motherhood as a condition of self-sufficient citizenship coincides with the rise of delayed parenthood among white, educated, middle-class women. According to demographic research, "mothers of newborns are older than their counterparts were two decades ago." Since 1990, the number of women ages 35–39 who are mothers of newborns increased 47 percent, and for women aged 40–44 the increase was 80 percent (Pew Research Social and Demographic Trends 2012). The Pew Center for Social and Demographic Trends states that the delay in the age of motherhood is associated with "delay in age of marriage and with growing educational attainment," with birth rates rising for the most educated women (those with at least some college education) and being "relatively stable for women with less education." Education is a crucial dimension of middle-class status, and the "more education a woman has, the later she tends to marry and have children," notes Pew. Conversely, although the birth rate for U.S. teens aged 15–19 has dropped in 16 of the past 18 years (the exceptions being 2006 and 2007) it remains much higher than in most industrialized countries (Congressional Research Service 2011). While teen childbearing is not "limited to teens in poverty," and its prevalence in the United States is "too high to be limited to a particular income group," research does indicate that a "disproportionate share of teen parents are from households with incomes either below poverty or just above poverty" (National Campaign to Prevent Teen and Unplanned Pregnancy 2009). Birth rates for Latino and African American teenagers are also significantly higher than those of other racial groups (Congressional Research Service 2011).

These statistics are worth citing in depth not because they explain teenage pregnancy, but because they construct and authorize the basis for norms and corrections that make their way into public–private initiatives and commercial reality productions. In the US, the "problem" of teenage pregnancy is closely tied to the perceived failure of young, working-class women and women of color to adopt current middle-class norms and expectations and practices. On 16 and Pregnant and Teen Mom, pregnancy is shown to be an "equal opportunity" problem that impacts girls across differences of race and class. This makes it possible to downplay the racial and class dimensions of teenage pregnancy and the whiteness and class privilege underlying childbearing norms. The denial of gender inequalities, meanwhile, is tied to the assumption that young women have achieved an unprecedented amount of freedom that must be managed properly. Angela McRobbie (2007) argues that having a "well-planned life" has become a requirement of femininity in neoliberal Western democracies. Increasingly, the notion of female empowerment hinges on the expectation that women pursue gainful employment and take charge of their fertility. What McRobbie calls a new sexual contract is underscored by a "posting" logic in which social movements (feminism, civil rights) are assumed to have done their jobs, and all women are assumed capable of achieving gender-blind notions of "independence and self-reliance." The paradox is that doing so involves endless "self-monitoring" and in times of stress "therapy, counseling or guidance," for now more than ever young women are "intensively managed subjects of post-feminist, gender-aware biopolitical practices of new governmentality," says McRobbie. Within this context, the concept of "planned parenthood" becomes an imperative to "avoid early maternity" in order to become financially self-sufficient and avoid State dependency (2007, 701). MTV's partnership with the National Campaign to Prevent Teen and Unwanted Pregnancy exemplifies these trends.

The Campaign was created in 1996 as a component of welfare reform legislation (no public funding was involved). Distancing itself from struggles over health care, control over one's body, access to abortion, funding for contraception and other issues emphasized by feminists and organizations such as Planned Parenthood, the nonprofit organization embarked on a mission of curbing teenage pregnancy in the service of "reducing out of wedlock births, improving family well being, reducing tax payers' burdens, reducing the need for abortion, reducing family turmoil and relationship conflict and helping women and men better plan their futures." This mission exemplifies a shift away from the moral condemnation of premarital sexual activity (especially for girls and women) to a focus on citizenship training. Building on Nikolas Rose's suggestion that "traditional codes of morality are in decline," giving way to a rising emphasis on "ethics or work on the self," Sara Bragg recognizes the progressive potentialities of an approach that invites young people to engage with themselves and take responsibility for their actions. However, she also cautions that the new "ethical" orientation of sex education, operating as it does within a neo-liberal context, may not serve girls well (2006, 548–549). In the wake of diminished social programs and public support systems, approaches to sex education that regulate the interiority of young women, "inviting the display of the self and experiences, can easily become part of the same technology through which self-regulating and responsible individuals are created rather than a critique of such practices" (2007, 549). The "at risk" girl shadows the "can do" (educated, sexually empowered, confident) girl and she is "more harshly stigmatized and judged for her failure in getting pregnant given the opportunities allegedly available to young women now," Bragg points out (2006, 548). If young women do not pursue adoption, they are further subjected to judgments, for as Ricki Solinger points out, an economic grid determines who is considered "fit" to be a mother, with only those women who can "afford to support a child . . . and pay for middle class advantages" thought to be appropriate consumers of "motherhood status" (1992/2000, 239).

Governmentality on these programs hinges less on formal expertise than on having "teens demonstrate to their peers how hard it is to become responsible for a baby before you're really responsible for yourself." On MTV, cameras "follow the young mothers-to-be as they make tough decisions about their lives, like dropping out of high school, either because it's too exhausting or to escape being gossiped about," and the viewer goes right into the delivery room, where plenty of "whimpers, gasps and grunts" convey the message that labor is painful. In the end, "pregnancy is the *easy* part—it's the parenthood that's really, really difficult," explains the National Campaign to Prevent Teen and Unwanted Pregnancy, and this point is magnified by take-away messages in which the female characters speak directly to the audience and televised therapy sessions with the cast after the episodes. It is assumed that, by showing the emotional, financial and physical difficulties of early childbearing, *16 and Pregnant* and *Teen Mom* will enable TV viewers (especially young women) to reflect on the costs, risks and challenges of getting pregnant, and plan their sexual behavior and life trajectories accordingly. To facilitate this, MTV also directs viewers to additional discussion questions, information, self-reflection exercises, educational games (such as My Paper Boyfriend) and other digital resources provided by the National Campaign to Prevent Teen and Unplanned Pregnancy and other organizations.

This citizenship training co-exists with a large swatch of MTV programming (including the reality programs *Jersey Shore* and *The Real World*) in which scantily clad young people hang around in hot tubs and on the beach, party and "hook up" on a casual basis, often with little reflection on birth control or life plans. Women bear the burden of these mixed messages, as they are the primary subjects of corrective initiatives adhering around the regulation of subjectivity and the female body. While the female subjects of 16 and Pregnant and Teen Mom often confess their failure to use birth control to parents and friends (one suspects these explanations are prompted by MTV), they are not shamed for having sex. MTV productions define the "problem" of teen pregnancy as a matter of improper life planning, and this message is emphasized in the public service announcements, therapy checkups, study guides and educational resources surrounding the shows. The aim is to encourage TV viewers to observe and evaluate others (even as they identify with these women as soap opera characters) as a lesson in the expectations of citizenship. We can see in the study guide for 16 and Pregnant, which translates the aims of authorities into the choices of individuals:

> Being a teen parent makes it a lot harder to reach your educational and financial goals. Is Gary ready to be the sole provider for his family? Will Amber be able to graduate from high school or go to college? More than half of teen moms never graduate from college and fewer than 2% finish college by age 30. How would it be different if they had waited a few more years before starting a family? Have you ever thought about how getting pregnant and having a baby might affect your future plans?

MTV does link the programs to websites (including It's Your Sex Life: http://kff.org/its-your-sex-life/) that provide information for avoiding pregnancy and about STD testing, and it has done this more as the seasons have progressed, but neither the cable network nor the National Campaign to Prevent Teen and Unplanned Pregnancy lobby to increase access to or public funding for contraception or reproductive health care. The objective is to encourage girls and young women to take responsibility for their futures, and the choices that are made available do not include abortion. Only one "very special" episode of 16 and Pregnant has dealt with abortion, and the various study materials downplay this option. Adoption, on the other hand, is advocated across the MTV programs and related shows like *I'm Having Their Baby* (2012) and *High School Moms* (2012).

Television's attempt to prevent teenage pregnancy perpetuates the assumption that only women with economic resources are fit to be parents. However, as with the obesity "epidemic," this message operates in tension with other logics of lifestyle. Tabloid magazines have helped make some *Teen Mom* participants into celebrities, and this attention has been difficult to reconcile with the stated anti-teen pregnancy mission. MTV reports regularly on the happenings of the *Teen Mom* stars through Facebook and other social media sites, and some of the participants (and their boyfriends) use Twitter and Facebook to chronicle their everyday activities and keep in touch with fans, bolstering their status as reality celebrities. Some have sought to use their exposure to launch careers in the entertainment industries. Cast member Farrah Abraham has been especially entrepreneurial in this regard, using social media extensively and even leaking a sex tape to bolster her celebrity. In 2015, Abraham landed a role on *Celebrity Big Brother* (2001–). Due to this media attention, the National Campaign and MTV have had to dispute accusations that they glamorize teenage childbearing and encourage girls to get pregnant for a chance to become famous. This anxiety points to a glaring tension in reality television's enlistment as birth control. On one hand, the productions promote normative life planning, taking real subjects as their material. On the other hand, their success as identifiable and emotional narratives relies on TV viewers' investments in the subjects who perform their lives on camera. At a time when ordinary people are encouraged to aspire to fame, and getting on reality TV or on the cover of a magazine is valued as another route to self-enterprising citizenship, the extent to which the "success" of the girls in becoming reality stars undermines their usefulness as "bad" subjects points to an unresolvable contradiction in reality television's governing ambitions.

NOTES

1 The term "logics of lifestyle" comes from Maureen Ryan (2015b), who points out that lifestyle television must be understood as a multifaceted phenomenon that intersects with, but cannot be reduced to, neoliberal rationalities.

2 My discussion of television and teenage pregnancy draws from my larger study, "It's Not TV, It's Birth Control," in *Reality Gendervision*, edited by Brenda Weber for Duke University Press. Many thanks to Brenda for also inviting me to deliver a keynote address to the Reality Gendervision conference at Indiana University. See Ouellette (2014b) for a more comprehensive and theoretical analysis of reality television, biopolitics, governmentality and young women.

4

THE LABOR OF LIFESTYLE

In June 2015, production on the third season of *Marriage Boot Camp* (2013–), a reality show that places couples in a mansion with marriage counselors to work on their relationships, ground to a halt when camera operators, grips, loggers and other behind-the-scenes workers walked off the job. Seeking better wages, health benefits and pensions, workers picketed outside the Los Angeles offices of Thinkfactory Media, the production company that produces *Marriage Boot Camp* for WE, a cable network targeting 18–49-year-old women with "real stories" about getting married, having children, raising a family and other situations that women are said to experience. The picketers demanded to be allowed to join the International Alliance of Theatrical Stage Employees (IATSE), a labor union that represents production and postproduction workers in theater, film and television (Patten and Robb 2015). Collective bargaining has a long history in Hollywood, where unions negotiate workplace conditions and employment contracts on behalf of everyone from actors to craft service workers. Because most reality productions are nonunionized, staff on productions like *Marriage Boot Camp* can be paid less, required to work overtime without pay, subjected to safety hazards, and denied medical and retirement benefits. Unlike writers of sitcoms and dramas, who are organized through the Writers Guild of America, "story editors," the term used to describe the writers of reality shows, are denied residual earnings on the cultural products they help to create.

Behind-the-scenes labor exploitation is hidden from the on-screen "reality" that is packaged and sold to TV viewers. The mechanics of production are concealed by commodity fetishism, defined by Marx as the erasure of labor power as the source of a commodity's value. "A commodity's market value depends on the erasure of the marks of production—any trace of the grime of the factory, the mass molding of the machine, and most of all, the exploitation of the worker," explains Laura Mulvey (1993, 10). Similarly, the market value of a cultural commodity such as *Marriage Boot Camp* hinges on the erasure of the labor of camera operators, editors, technicians and caterers. However, the cost-efficient mode of production associated with reality and lifestyle entertainment also exemplifies a shift away from the stable Fordist factory, toward the flexible and contingent labor associated with postindustrial capitalism. Encouraged by the demise of public interest rules and deregulatory policies, the proliferation of channels, and rising production costs, the TV industry has come to rely on amateur talent and nonunionized and freelance production crews that can be mobilized quickly and who are often denied benefits and long-term employment contracts (Raphael 2009).

While the labor of producing television is concealed from what we see on our TV sets, reality and lifestyle formats often take work—broadly defined—as a narrative theme. Many programs revolve around the unwaged and waged labor associated with producing lifestyle, transforming the self, home, body, family and psyche, and achieving the "good life." For example, self-help oriented interventions like *Marriage Boot Camp* present work on the self as a solution to an array of problems, from relationship discord to unemployment. This type of programming often targets female audiences who are assumed to be the primary caretakers of the private sphere, the family and the home, as well as the managers of their careers. Even though most women work outside the home, domestic how-to programs have flourished on broadcast and cable television, circulating advice, regimens and resources for perfecting "women's work," or historically feminized forms of unpaid domestic labor such as cooking, housekeeping, caretaking and childrearing. Beauty and style makeover programs, meanwhile, connect the normally invisible labor of making and remaking femininity to goals ranging from staging the perfect wedding (*Bridalplasty*, 2010–2011; *Brides*

Gone Styled, 2015–) to competing in a postindustrial workforce that increasingly expects people to look "attractive and stylish" (McRobbie 2002, 102).

Recent years have also witnessed an explosion of programming about workplaces and careers. Many of these programs revolve around "creative" and glamorous occupations that present an alternative to the "alienating grind of the office or factory" (Mueller 2012). Labor is enacted on these shows as an extension of identity and self-actualization, not as a monetary exchange between workers and employees. Programs revolving around the skills and routines of stylists, designers and top chefs take TV viewers behind the scenes of glamorized lifestyle industries. These programs highlight the mediation of meanings, tastes, aspirations, beauty norms and brands, and narrate the route to success in occupations where workers are motivated by creativity and "passion," and work is often indistinguishable from leisure. Productions about hairdressers, manicurists, tanning salon personnel, fitness instructors and other ordinary aesthetic workers have also proliferated, treating modestly paid service-sector work as an extension of glamour labor and creative labor. Meanwhile, competitions to determine the next top model, celebrity chef or design star fuse the conventions of the talent show with the unpaid internship. On these shows, creative work is enacted as a meritocracy in which the most talented, ambitious and self-enterprising can rise to the top, and perhaps even command a TV program of their own. Doubling as promotions for television networks and brands integrated into the storylines, competitions exude a "new spirit of capitalism" (Boltanski and Chiapello 2007) in which labor is performed, often for free, in the service of creativity, self-actualization and future economic outcomes (Ross 2010).

This chapter situates the *labor of lifestyle* enacted on popular nonfiction and reality formats within the conditions of work in postindustrial capitalist societies. This context is not limited to paid employment, but encompasses unwaged forms of labor that reproduce social life and generate new forms of economic value. I also situate the labor involved in the manufacture of lifestyle, and the rising visibility of cultural and aesthetic workers on television, within debates over the "creative industries" as a model for work in the twenty-first century. Critically unpacking the types of labor performed on screen, I argue that reality and lifestyle offer an informal tutorial for learning to labor at a time when the conditions and expectations of work are changing. As we will see, struggles behind the scenes in the TV industry, and lessons about the changing demands and rewards of work circulated through popular nonfiction and reality programming, are equally connected to the labor politics of postindustrial capitalist societies.

WOMEN'S WORK: AFFECTIVE LABOR

Reality and lifestyle television addresses women as self-sufficient "subjects of capacity" who are assumed to earn their own living, participate in consumer culture, reflect on their choices, and take responsibility for their situations (McRobbie 2010). As Angela McRobbie points out, media culture tends to assume that the struggle for gender equality has already been achieved, leaving individual women free to choose their destinies. Feminist critics question this postfeminist logic, noting that women still earn only 78 cents on the male dollar, and that increased access to education, work and other domains is still uneven and partial. Another point of contention is the sexual division of labor in the home. Sociologists point out that even as women have entered the paid workforce en masse, and are held "equally accountable" to the historically male breadwinner ethic (Fraser and Gordon 1997), they still perform a disproportionate share of affective and familial labor in the home. This activity constitutes a "second shift" of labor that is performed for free (Hochschild 1989/2003).

Reality and lifestyle programs about homemaking, interior decorating, parenting, cooking, cleaning and "wife swapping" perpetuate the division of labor by assuming that women are responsible for the care of homes and families. What scholars call *affective labor* is not limited to domestic chores, but encompasses a range of emotional, caring and maternal labor tasks performed "naturally" by women within families. This care work is an "act that, for the most part, women do; it is a gendered activity" (Meyer 2000, 6). While affective labor is not compensated, feminists have long characterized "women's work" as foundational to the social reproduction of capitalism (Spigel 1992). More recently, the social theorist Michael Hardt has theorized women's caring and kin work as a bottom-up dimension of biopower, indispensable to the "emerging forces of governmentality to create, manage, and control populations—the power to manage life" (Hardt 1999, 98). Following this formulation, it seems clear that women's domestic and affective labor is crucial to the self-sufficiency and well being of individuals and families, a role that, as we saw in earlier chapters, has become more urgent in light of neoliberal trends such as the State's retreat from social service provision.

While the sexual division of labor is not as rigid as it was a few decades ago, a "gender segregation" of tasks still occurs (Swenson 2009) and women continue to perform more affective and household labor than men (Hochschild 1989/2003). Lifestyle programs legitimate this arrangement by gendering expertise and aligning women's path to self-actualization with assumed domestic and caretaking duties. As Rebecca Swenson demonstrates in her research on The Food Network, cooking shows hosted by female cooks are usually more practical in nature and are often set inside the home (or on a studio set designed to resemble a home kitchen). Aired mainly during the day, they present cooking as a labor of love that is done by women for families. Cooking shows hosted by men, on the other hand, are more apt to appear during primetime, be set in professional kitchens and treat cooking as a leisure activity, an intellectual pursuit or a competitive sport (2009, 40–41). Male TV personalities like Mario Batali (Molto Mario, 1996–2010), Emeril Lagasse (Emeril Live, 1997–2010) and Alton Brown (Good Eats, 1999–2012) are more likely to mention their professional culinary training and wear formal chef attire; female personalities, exemplified by Rachel Ray (30-Minute Meals, 2001–), Giada De Laurentiis (Everyday Italian, 2003–), Ina Garten (Barefoot Contessa, 2002–) and self-proclaimed "domestic goddess" Nigella Lawson (Nigella Bites, 2000–2007; Nigella Kitchen, 2010), are more likely to come across as "approachable," wear aprons, and "prepare meals for friends and family members rather than as professional chefs or artists" (2009, 43–44).

Many instructional lifestyle programs promise to help women manage a second shift of labor in the home with greater style and efficiency. While some (disproportionately white and middle class) women have gained access to high-profile careers and public life, the home is still gendered as the "natural" sphere for women, and lifestyle programs that revolve around domestic pursuits perpetuate this assumption. However, they do so in clever ways that encourage TV viewers to embrace stylized and professionalized approaches to homemaking and caretaking as a personal choice, not an unequal burden. As Elizabeth Nathanson argues, the pleasures and rewards of choosing the private home as a site of "love and fulfillment" are emphasized over the lingering gender inequalities responsible for the second shift (2013, 11). Of course, the choice of domestic labor as a "privileged form of leisure" is available only to those women who can afford to invest time and money in the activities demonstrated on television. The experiences of working-class women who cannot afford these luxuries (and who may clean houses and care for children for wages) are marginalized on homemaking programs (2013, 21). While the lack of affordable daycare options, onsite childcare centers and adequate parental leave policies in the US contributes to the gendered second shift (Hochschild 1989/2003), lifestyle programs avoid these societal issues. Instead, the women courted by upscale cable lifestyle networks, who are "expected to juggle a successful family life with an equally successful professional career," are offered a plethora of options for managing "time crunches." While rooted more in fantasy than reality, the endless tips and techniques for "saving time" on domestic labor reinforce the idea that women can "do it all" (Nathanson 2013, 5).

For example, cooking shows aimed at women recognize that their time is extremely limited, and present "time-saving" methods for preparing healthy and delicious family meals, says Nathanson. Programs like 30 Minute Meals, which launched the successful Rachel Ray brand, promote "domestic efficiency and multi-tasking," showing how "women can incorporate skills learned in the workplace into their kitchens" (2013, 22). Parenting advice programs like Supernanny (2005–2012) dramatize the "costs families pay when women's attention is divided" between home and work, and promise to solve these dilemmas swiftly and efficiently through expertise and daily regimens that combine women's "natural" parenting instincts with professional techniques similar to running a business. Perhaps no problem on lifestyle television has come to exemplify the time crunch that women in postfeminist societies experience more than clutter. As Nathanson points out, entire programs now revolve around the need to make "the home more useful by imposing order on what appears to be chaos." On shows like Home Made Simple (2011–) and Mission: Organization (2003–) chaos manifests as problems like household disorganization, "unattractive" interior aesthetics and dysfunctional layouts—"problems that can be solved through new consumer products and experts who teach the merits of simplicity and streamlining" (Nathanson 2013, 28).

Cleaning programs like *Clean House* (2003–2011) and *How Clean Is Your House?* (2004–2011) take the problem of clutter a step further by suggesting that "once functional homes have fallen into a state of mess and filth and need to be restored to their former state, crucial to family health." As a variation on the makeover format, these shows revolve around failed homemakers and professional experts who diagnose the crux of the problem and supervise a transformation culminating in a dramatic reveal. Grandmotherly housecleaning specialists wearing high heels and white lab coats save the day with new methods for combatting dirt and disarray that combine age-old household hints with streamlined corporate efficiency (Nathanson 2013, 38). The entertainment appeal hinges on the combination of voyeurism, identification and spectacle that many reality shows provide. While the cases presented are extreme, the message that all women can manage the burden of the double shift with a streamlined new housekeeping regimen prevails, as suggested by the tie-in books, DVDs and other merchandise based on the shows.

Figure 4.1 *How Clean Is Your House?* plays on anxieties about women's inability to keep up with a "second shift" of labor in the home.

Self-help interventions also invite women to take responsibility for the care and well being of their families, and circulate resources (expertise, regimens, products) to help them do so. Just as homemaking programs infuse domestic work with techniques from the business world, self-help programs bring corporate strategies into the emotional and therapeutic work that women are expected to perform on behalf of spouses and families. This tendency to infuse women's affective labor with an enterprising ethic and techniques of the self modeled on cost–benefit calculations, auditing and other business strategies is exemplified by the bestselling self-help book *Spousonomics: Using Economics to Master Love, Marriage and Dirty Dishes* (Szuchman and Anderson 2011), which teaches women to empower themselves by "applying economic concepts to the domestic front." The authors have appeared on many advice programs aimed at women, including the daytime *Rachel Ray* show (2006–), where they presented "strategies borrowed from Wall Street" as the "secret to domestic bliss." Applying an economic grid to feminized forms of women's work seems more compatible with historically male-coded ideals of self-mastery, self-maximization and self-enterprise that have gained currency as a basis for personhood across social differences.

As Micki McGee points out, the "labors of women's daily lives" have historically been incompatible with self-help programs. The very idea of "self-invention and self-mastery hails from a culture where someone else's labors (that of wives and enslaved persons) would provide for the necessities of everyday life," she contends (2005, 9). As the self-help genre has become more aligned with the discourses and policies of neoliberalism, it has embraced economic metaphors and goals like "winning" in life have been difficult to reconcile with the caretaking demands associated with family and childrearing. "Caring for others constitutes a significant problem for the entrepreneurial bottom line unless one is willing to imagine the home as part of one's market calculations, factored into one's personal profit-and-loss statement," explains McGee (87). Televised interventions like *Marriage Boot Camp* help manage this tension by giving an "enterprise form" to the so-called haven in a heartless world (Ouellette and Wilson 2011).

The Dr. Phil self-help brand, which encompasses a television program as well as dozens of tie-in books, workbooks, DVDs and a website, exemplifies the application of market rationalities to marriage, parenting and family.

Dr. Phil products translate corporate practicum and skill into strategies for achieving the "results" women are assumed to want as wives, mothers and the "CEOs of their families." Scholars have traced how women's affective labor has been dislocated from the familial realm and transformed into commodities for sale and postindustrial job requirements. Nurses, flight attendants, coffee shop baristas and other service-sector workers are expected to perform emotional labor and provide customer "care," on top of other job duties. Likewise, people who serve as amateur talent on reality docusoaps, including the *Real Housewives* franchise (2006–), are expected to perform "authentic" emotions and exude personality in the service of melodrama and ratings (Grindstaff and Murray 2015). The Dr. Phil brand exemplifies the reverse trend—the diffusion of market logic into unwaged affective labor performed in the home. Coaching belabored women to practice "emotional management" and "caring with currency," Dr. Phil and his ilk do not challenge the double shift but rather recast women's work as an entrepreneurial—and therefore masculinized and "empowering"— activity. Following this model, interventions from *Supernanny* and *Parents Just Don't Understand* (2014–) to *Mission Makeover* (2009–) and *Fix My Life* (2012–) invite women to "maximize" their affective capacities without de-gendering kin work (Ouellette and Wilson 2011). In this way, reality and lifestyle television not only legitimates unpaid women's work, it enlists women to "choose" the sexual division of labor as a path to enterprising personhood.

KEEPING UP APPEARANCES: AESTHETIC LABOR

Much reality and lifestyle television fixates on improving the way women dress, wear their hair, apply their makeup and comport their bodies. Self-improvement is closely associated with the gendered markers of beauty and style, and the makeover format in particular is devoted to transforming the way women look. Experts enlist participants in guided self-work regimens in the service of goals such as appearing more feminine and "respectable" (*Ladette to Lady*, 2005–2010; *Charm School*, 2007–2009) losing weight (*Mission Makeover*, 2009–) and finding romantic partners (*Tough Love*, 2009–2013). This message is hardly new: Since the early 1900s, women's magazines have circulated advice, regimens and products for perfecting femininity, conveying the idea that women must be constantly concerned about how they "appear" to others (Berger 1972/1990), while also emphasizing women's active role in producing themselves as desirable feminine subjects. Much beauty and style advice is geared to the performance of idealized femininity, a process that reflects gender norms and involves perpetual self-scrutiny and work (Butler 1990; Gill 2007). While the pressure to make and remake femininity is connected to gender inequalities, it is also a form of labor: improving and transforming the body through exercise, waxes, dieting, teeth whitening, grooming, blow outs and beauty regimens, as well as through carefully chosen wardrobes and accessories, requires time and effort as well as financial resources. Often presented as an investment in oneself, this unwaged labor is linked by popular media to a range of potential payoffs, from upward mobility through romance to success in the workplace.

As Angela McRobbie observes, recent decades have seen a burgeoning culture of "pampering yourself," with a wide range of beauty treatments marketed not only as a requirement of normative femininity, but also as a "resource to be mined for added values which can enhance performance in the workplace." This "added value" is especially important in the expanding service sector, which has replaced manufacturing as a source of low- and mid-level employment, and which increasingly "expects its workforce to look especially attractive and stylish for what is called aesthetic labor" (2002, 100). Aesthetic labor refers to the process of monitoring, screening and improving one's physical appearance (Mears 2014) in compliance with the expectations of employers, and is widespread in the service and retail industries. Corporations like Abercrombie & Fitch and Gap expect their store employees to embody corporate ideals of physical attractiveness and stylishness. Aesthetic labor can also be undertaken as a means to advance in careers or gain entry into a new field. Aspiring fashion models are an obvious example, but many cultural occupations—including the gig of reality TV participant—place a higher value on workers who are camera ready, and embody youth, grooming and aesthetic style. Increasingly, aesthetic labor has also become part of self-imaging practices, especially among young women (Gill, Scharff and Elias 2016). The imperative to monitor and control one's appearance in accordance with idealized norms seeps into the way women and girls photograph themselves for social media, and the imperative to produce an attractive self-image is connected to rise of self-branding discussed in earlier chapters. This quest to produce a socially marketable image of oneself can be observed on reality shows like *Keeping Up With the Kardashians* (2007–) and *Rich Kids of Beverly Hills* (2014–), whose fashion and style-conscious female cast members routinely discuss and debate the aesthetic qualities of their selfies and use social platforms like Instagram to brand themselves as feminine role models.

Women have historically been called upon to discipline their bodies, work on their physical "imperfections" and stylize their appearances more than men, but this is changing somewhat as manufacturing gives way to service work in Western capitalist societies and men are called upon to perform aesthetic labor as well. On makeover programs, a major impetus to learn what to wear, lose weight or erase ten years from one's appearance is to achieve job security. As "jobs for life" have given way to flexible and contingent employment contracts, and labor unions have lost power, becoming and remaining employable has become a permanent process that requires constant retraining and self-work on the part of men as well as women (McGee 2005). What's more, the transition from industrial factory production to postindustrial service work as the "mainstay of employment for most people in capitalist societies" requires that everyone adopt characteristics (including nurturance and "to be looked-at ness") that have historically been understood as female, notes Valerie Walkerdine (2003, 238–240). What has long been demanded of women—to be "adaptable, desirable, presentable, consumable"—has been intensified and extended throughout the workforce. In this respect, Walkerdine points out, keeping up with the shifting demands and expectations of a precarious postindustrial workforce has much in common with the endless labor of making and remaking femininity (2003, 238–240; Ouellette and Hay 2008).

The makeover formats that swept television in the early 2000s, including *Queer Eye for the Straight Guy* (2003–2007) and *What Not to Wear* (2003–2013), established rationales and conventions for monitoring and improving people's appearances while TV cameras rolled. Experts scrutinize the bodies, fashion choices and style quotients of ordinary people and present resources (surgery, salon visits, exercise regimens, advice, products) for transformation. Women are the mainstay of makeovers, but men are also targeted—often for work-related reasons. Indeed, for both men and women, the impetus for undergoing the surveillance and scrutiny of fashion and style experts is often connected to the desire to pursue a dream job, advance at work or simply avoid downsizing (Sender 2005; Ouellette and Hay 2008; Weber 2009). *The Fairy Job Mother* (2010), a self-help intervention that tackles soaring unemployment rates triggered by the financial crisis of the late 2000s and the recession that followed, is an especially clear example. On this show, the unemployed are required to undergo makeovers (including new hairstyles and wardrobe fixes) as well as employment counseling. The notion that a makeover can fix a problem rooted in a changing economy is egregious, but not surprising. Today, we are all expected to participate in aesthetic labor to varying degrees. Instead of recognizing ourselves as workers with common struggles and collective bargaining power, we are encouraged to operate as entrepreneurs of the self who must use the resources at our disposal (including television) to navigate the rising uncertainties—and potential rewards—of contemporary work (Rose 1996; Walkerdine 2003).

Given the rising demands of aesthetic labor, it is no wonder that the beauty and style industries (hair, tanning, nails, cosmetics, fitness, personal styling) have boomed in recent decades.[1] While makeover programs assist with the aesthetic labor we perform on ourselves, another burgeoning strand of reality programming revolves around workers who provide beauty and spa treatments, tanning sessions, haircuts, manicures, exercise classes, personal shopping other aesthetic services. These shows take aesthetic industries as settings for reality entertainment steeped in emotion, interpersonal drama and suspense, and tend not to dwell on the mundane or exploitative aspects of the jobs they profile. Hair salons (*The Salon*, 2003–2004; *Blow Out*, 2004–2006; *LA Hair*, 2012– ; *Houston Beauty*, 2013), nail salons (*Nail Files*, 2011–2013), tanning parlors (*Sunset Tan*, 2007–2008), fitness clubs (*Work Out*, 2006–2008; *Work Out New York*, 2015) and personal shopping businesses (*Million Dollar Shopper*, 2013) set the stage for a range of formats from docusoaps to talent competitions. On the bright side, these programs make visible, and indeed celebrate, the normally hidden, devalued, low-paid and feminized labor of aestheticizing consumers for pay. They showcase the creativity, ingenuity, craft and skill involved in beauty and style work. For a medium that has long overrepresented upscale professionals and stigmatized blue-collar and pink-collar workers, this is a potentially progressive move.

However, people who work at salons, gyms and retail stores are part of the postindustrial workforce. As such, they must perpetually work on and invest in their own appearances, as well as navigate increasingly insecure working conditions where health insurance and pension plans are no longer the norm. Most aesthetic laborers are nonunionized and only modestly paid at best. These issues are downplayed on reality television, where the labor of providing aesthetic services is celebrated as glamorous and creative. This tendency is not unique to TV, but cuts across the policy and creative industry discourse as well. Hair work is a case in point. According to the U.S. Bureau of Labor Statistics, employment for hair stylists in the United States is expected to grow by 12.7 percent; rising consumer demand to "receive extensions, hair color, straightening and more could translate to as many as 77,600 new cosmetologist positions by 2022." While *US News and World Report's 2014 Guide to Best Jobs* acknowledges that most hairdressers aren't salaried employees, that many work part-time, and that the median hourly wage was only $11.12 (or $23,140 per year), it casts the occupation as a cool job for creative types: whether they're "forming beehives or braids, dreadlocks or ducktails, ponytails or pompadours, hairdressers are maestros of styling . . . And just like many of the professions on this year's list of Best Jobs, hairdressing is more than a career. It's a calling."

The tendency to embellish aesthetic labor as a creative calling exemplifies the wider celebration of what economists call *creative industries*. In his much-debated book *The Rise of the Creative Class*, Richard Florida (2002) characterizes a range of so-called creative workers, from designers to new media workers, as constituting a vanguard new class. These workers, he argues, are more satisfied than traditional factory or office workers because they have more decision-making opportunities and venues for self-expression. In a chapter called "The Machine Shop versus the Hair Salon," Florida claims that if offered a choice between a well-paying job with benefits and long-term security at a machine shop and a lower-paying job with fewer benefits and more risks at a hair salon, most people will choose to work at the hair salon. This, he says, is because styling hair, unlike Fordist machine labor, is a "creative" occupation that allows for a higher degree of flexibility, artistry, entrepreneurialism and autonomy. Business writer Virginia Postrel (2004) agrees. Citing Florida, Postrel argues that, as capitalism and everyday life have become more aestheticized and "demand for style experts and aesthetic workers has exploded," new career options have opened up for people who might once have pursued less expressive crafts, like waitresses or truck drivers. Aesthetic labor like hair styling, which was once considered an "effeminate and low-prestige" profession, will become more desirable and prestigious as more people seek out creative occupations, she contends (2004, 180–181). These arguments conflate aesthetic labor like hairstyling with more highly compensated creative jobs (such as computer designer) and suggest that, for those who can be expressive at work, creativity is its own reward.

Reality television reproduces this creative industries discourse by presenting service-oriented aesthetic labor as a reward onto itself. Issues like wages and benefits are minimized and instead the labor of aestheticizing consumers is narrated as an alluring opportunity for self-actualization. This is accomplished by dusting the ordinary work routines of spas, salons and fitness centers with a large dose of glamour and celebrity. The proliferation of shows about hairdressers is a telling case in point. The glamorization of hairstyling was set in motion when the landmark British series *The Salon* (2003–2004) built a fully operational hair salon on a television studio stage equipped with twenty cameras and thirty microphones. Hair stylists and other aesthetic workers (masseuses, manicurists) were hired to double as service providers and amateur talent for the TV show, and the public was invited to come in for haircuts and beauty treatments (spray tans, manicures, massage, waxing, Botox, permanent makeup applications), while TV viewers looked on five days a week. The opening to the program doubled as a public relations campaign for the hairstyling industry. TV viewers were informed that British consumers made "more than 300 million visits to salons and spas each year, spending £4.1 billion pounds annually." While hairdressers were acknowledged to earn only £300 pounds per week on average (roughly $470 US), the hair salon was pitched as an exceptionally alluring and potentially profitable workplace: "Hairdressing is not just about perms and blue rinses," insisted the narrator, it is "glamorous," "exciting," "passionate," "sexy," "challenging" and "cool," explained the program. With the power to "change the way we look and feel," hairdressers are becoming "demi-gods" who enjoy an unprecedented new "level of celebrity." At a minimum, especially talented and ambitious stylists could earn ten times the amount of the average hairdresser, claimed the show, and enjoy a glamorous lifestyle signified by "fancy cars" and trendy clothes.

In the US, shows about hairdressers are usually set in posh salons in places like Beverly Hills and New York City. The owners are often billed as "celebrity stylists" who attract a wealthy, star-studded clientele and enjoy considerable notoriety of their own. While most star sightings on these shows involve D-list celebrities or former child stars, the link to Hollywood is continually evoked to make aesthetic labor alluring. Salon work is also legitimated through associating a historically feminized and queer industry with "manly" heterosexual men. While gay men have long been depicted as natural "style mavens," due in part to their perceived association with hip urban style and femininity (Lewis 2008), reality television has made a point to cast heterosexual men as upscale stylists. Unlike traditional barbers, these men exude a personal style, work in aestheticized settings and have female as well as male clients. At a time when traditionally male-coded industrial jobs are declining in the West, The Salon made a point to feature white, clearly identified heterosexual men as trendsetting hairstylists, conveying the idea that aesthetic labor has transcended women's work. In the US, Blow Out followed a "defiantly straight" male celebrity hairstylist in Beverly Hills, who later became a judge on Shear Genius (2007–2010), a competition to crown the "best hairstylist in America" that provides the winner with an apprenticeship with the Nexus company and a chance to style hair for a photo shoot in Allure magazine; many other programs have followed suit. Reality programs also lend prestige to aesthetic labor by casting hairdressers not as "ball and chain" workers, but as entrepreneurs of the self who are passionate about their calling. Indeed, TV hairstylists are shown to possess the attributes of the ideal postindustrial worker—flexibility, adaptability, creativity, aestheticization and entrepreneurialism.

As Gavin Mueller (2012) points out, television paints a sharp contrast between blue-collar labor, which is coded as white, male, working-class, exhausting and "grizzled" on shows like American Trucker (2011), Deadliest Catch (2005–), Dirty Jobs (2005–2012) and Coal (2011), and postindustrial

Figure 4.2 Male hairdressers regularly compete in the hairstyling competition *Shear Genius.*

cultural work, which is presented as creative, youthful, energetic and multicultural. This is exemplified, he says, by talent competitions among aspiring celebrity chefs, interior designers, fashion designers, models, editorial assistants, pop stars, brand ambassadors and other creative workers, which feature "young diverse creative in hip urban locales." According to Mueller, reality television's tendency to favor the latter programs is no surprise, given that "cultural work is what remains of aspirational middle class careers for Americans, who live in a country where two-thirds of exports are cultural goods and intellectual property." Nobody, it is assumed, expects to achieve upward mobility by driving trucks, hauling garbage or mining coal. Aesthetic labor—from styling hair to supervising tanning beds—has been folded into the definition of creative work by analysts and the TV industry, and the hair salon is presented as a hip, stimulating and diverse environment for the marriage of creativity and entrepreneurialism. Salon work is presented as an equal opportunity for everyone to pursue entry into the celebrated "creative class" regardless of gender, class, ethnicity, race or sexual orientation.

This message "posts" social inequalities by assuming that society has overcome the racism, sexism, classism and homophobia of the past. As with the programming discussed in earlier chapters, salon shows imply that individuals are now free to choose their identities and determine their own destinies. The political history of aesthetic labor, and the salon's relationship to disadvantaged groups (such as women and African Americans) is discounted and erased. For example, a number of programs revolving around African American hair stylists, including LA Hair and Cutting It In the ATL (2015–), highlight black beauty ideals, and the creativity and skills involved in realizing them. However, none of these programs addresses the history of the black beauty shop, which has historically played a role in nurturing African American communities and facilitating the aims of the civil rights movement (Willett 2000; Gil 2001, 2010). While the talents and enterprising skills of stylists are often celebrated, the extent to which the nascent beauty industries—including early hair salons—presented rare opportunities for both white and African American women's financial autonomy and entrepreneurialism is unaddressed. For example, LA Hair, which follows an African American female celebrity hairstylist who operates a high-end salon in Los Angeles, plays up the excitement that ensues when a famous (or quasi-famous) African American patron comes in. Working at the salon is presented as a lucky opportunity for stargazed stylists whose personal creativity, passion and self-enterprise is spontaneously rewarded (wages, tips and benefits are never mentioned). Even as a frazzled stylist repeatedly falls asleep at the hair-washing sink because she is exhausted from traveling from job to job to service wealthy clients at home, the owner insists that she step up to the challenge and "stop sabotaging" her success. At a time when the black-owned neighborhood beauty parlor is giving way to corporate chains, LA Hair and similar shows celebrate multiculturalism and individual success, but gloss over the racial politics of postindustrial work.

The stakes of casting hair stylists as entrepreneurs of the self who channel their passion into profits is made clear on Houston Beauty, a docusoap set in a vocational beauty school with a predominantly low-income, African American and Latino student body. Unlike luxury salon docusoaps, the setting is grimly institutional. Elderly instructors demonstrate skills on well-worn mannequins in fluorescent-lit classrooms with peeling paint. Pupils who drop in and out of the program based on the availability of financial aid, and who sometimes sleep in their cars, converse about their passion for cosmetology and ambition to become "celebrity stylists," often referencing TV programs they've seen. Besides mastering technical skills like hair cutting, weaving and makeup application, they are taught "self-discipline" by the stern instructors and incited to perform weekly challenges (such as producing commercials for the school) that are likely devised by the show's producers. The students who provide free talent for the reality production are unlikely to overcome the structural conditions of extreme poverty and racial inequality, let alone gain access to the glamorous high-end salons, celebrity clients and personal fame depicted on television. Yet, the surge of reality shows about the creative and glamorous world of hairdressers conveys the assumption that anything is possible—and perpetuates the notion that if they fail they have no one but themselves to blame.

Even the notoriously exploitative nail industry has been cast on television as a self-expressive, celebrity-studded place to work. Journalists and advocacy groups have exposed the low wages, meager tips, unpaid apprenticeships, and racial and ethnic hierarchies experienced by manicurists. Many of the female workers interviewed for a *New York Times* expose of the city's burgeoning nail industry reported working long hours without job security or benefits, and the average wage hovered around $35 a day, or $3 an hour. On top of this, manicurists were exposed to health risks associated with the toxic chemicals used in nail products, including chronic migraines, respiratory problems and miscarriages; as advocacy groups were quick to point out, hair salon workers are also exposed to health risks (Maslin Nir 2015). None of these issues are discussed on *Nail Files*, a show set in a "celebrity" salon called The Painted Nail. We don't learn what the manicurists and pedicurists earn, whether they receive health benefits, or if toxic chemicals are used in the services they provide. Instead, we see the Latina manicurists servicing minor celebrities, gossiping and accusing one another of stealing tips in scenes clearly staged for the camera, while the white salon owner attempts to build her brand and develop a merchandise line. The competition *Nail'd It* (2014–), on the other hand, pits aspiring "nail artists" against one another as they "compete for recognition and a cash prize." Here again, the recognition of women's creativity and skills occurs in tandem with the intensification of aesthetic labor and the glamorization of low-paid service work.

Tellingly, programs about the aesthetic service sector now have their own version of the makeover. *Tabatha's Salon Takeover* (2008–2013) opens by informing TV viewers that most salons (with the exception of chains) fail within three years of opening, and promises to turn around flagging and "at risk" businesses. Each week, Tabatha Coffey, a "renowned" hairstylist and salon owner who competed on *Shear Genius*, sets up shop at a failing salon, diagnoses the problem and implements a plan for change. In addition to restyling the aesthetics of the salon, she teaches salon owners to manage "through creativity" and stylists to take ownership of their performance and sales. In a typical episode, she coaches an owner on the brink of bankruptcy to stop micromanaging and sets about reforming a staff that had "lost its passion." She places surveillance cameras in the salon and reviews the secret footage she collects with the workers before firing several stylists and coaching the rest to promote the business—and themselves—with greater enthusiasm. In another episode, the postracial logic endemic to shows about hairstylists is made explicit when Tabatha attempts to turn around an African American salon in a rapidly gentrifying Nashville neighborhood. Florida's endorsement of creative industries hinges in part on his claim that cities with the most creative workers enjoy better economies and quality of life indices. While Coffey does not use this language, she proceeds to reinvent the salon, its owner and its workers with the goal of accommodating and capitalizing on the white creative professionals who are moving into the historically working-class, African American neighborhood. To do so, she deploys harsh tactics (such as shaming, surveillance and humiliation) familiar from beauty and style makeover shows, especially when working-class individuals and people of color are the targets. According to Coffey, it is up to the owner and her staff to rise to the challenge of the city's changing economy: they must "step up, be responsible" and "embrace the diverse wave of the future." By making over workers whose aesthetic labor is integral to the rising imperative to "look right" on the job, *Tabatha's Salon Takeover* brings television's engagement with beauty and style full circle.

ALL WORK ALL THE TIME: IMMATERIAL LABOR

While reality programs glamorize aesthetic labor, they also reveal the extension of work into personal time. As Vicki Mayer argues, the term "precariat" refers to knowledge and creative workers who "lose the power to negotiate the value of their work time." As the nature of work becomes increasingly flexible, insecure and fragmented, life and labor become less differentiated. Work is subsumed into "off hours" through the need to be in touch with work through digital technologies and the expectation that social activities that flow into the evenings and weekends (including social networking) are an investment in one's career or even a informal job requirement (2014, 67). On television, the demands of all work, all the time are narrated as a choice that creative professionals who love their jobs are happy to embrace. For example, reality shows revolving around fashion stylists show them living and breathing their jobs as an extension of their identities and lifestyles.

There are many docusoaps and talent competitions revolving around fashion stylists who dress and accessorize the rich and famous, aestheticize people and products for magazine and advertising shoots, and prepare A-list stars for the red carpet (Glam God with Vivica A. Fox, 2008; The City, 2009; Styl'd, 2009; Hollywood Unzipped: Stylist Wars, 2012; Styled by June, 2012; B.O.R.N. to Style, 2014–). Many are cast as celebrities in their own right, who command media attention, travel the world, hobnob with movie stars, and oversee personal brands and merchandise lines. Rachel Zoe of The Rachel Zoe Project (2008–2013) has achieved particular notoriety, and her influence reverberates well beyond television. For example, career guides and vocational programs aimed at aspiring stylists acknowledge that styling is a competitive field and often recommend the low-paid retail clothing and personal shopping industries as a launching pad, but they routinely celebrate Zoe as a success story. The Rachel Zoe Project also operates as a career manual of sorts, taking TV viewers behind the scenes of the styling business and showing what it takes to succeed in a "cool job in a hot industry" (Neff, Wissinger and Zukin 2005).

The show chronicled Zoe's styling business over five seasons, with storylines revolving around Fashion Week, dressing stars for awards shows, magazine and advertising shoots, and product launches. Amidst the drama of missing Fed Ex packages, bickering staff and the race to procure the perfect red carpet dress, Zoe indulges in shopping sprees and tries (often unsuccessfully) to juggle her career with her personal life. While she was running her stylist business and filming for Bravo, she also worked as a brand ambassador for retailers like Piperlime and Shoedazzle. Her job, which was incorporated into the storylines, was to sift through hundreds of online products and provide recommendations; her "picks" reportedly sold out in hours. In 2001, the *Hollywood Reporter* ranked Zoe number one on its list of the Top 25 Stylists in America. With aspirations to design, Zoe launched clothing, handbag and accessories lines for high-end department stores and the mass-market QVC while TV cameras rolled. Driven by "passion," her work was virtually inseparable from her private life. On the show, she often works to the point of physical exhaustion, dashing around to fashion shows and photo shoots, attending to her clients, scouring look books and building her fashion brand. Even socializing is work—chats with designers, shopping and attending parties are all part of the job of generating exposure for herself and celebrity clientele. In the early seasons, Zoe operated her freelance business out of her apartment, which enabled her to work 24/7. The supersized Starbucks coffee cup she carries at all times is an entirely convincing product placement.

Shows like *The Rachel Zoe Project* present work as an opportunity for self-actualization. Aesthetic labor is enacted as a chosen way of life, in which creativity, entrepreneurialism and self-making are intertwined. But they also make visible the demands of creative labor—the dedifferentiation of work and leisure, uncertainty, the investment of money and time, the sheer exhaustion of "crunch time." Indeed, scholars describe creative workers as the "shock absorbers" of the postindustrial economy. From fashion modeling to new media design, workers in so-called creative industries are expected to work long hours, devote off hours to honing their craft and developing a portfolio, and "accept risks previously mediated by firms (such as business cycle fluctuations and market failures)" (Neff et al. 2005). Hailed as "model entrepreneurs" by industry and government, creative workers are exemplars of the "move away from stable notions of 'career' to more informal, insecure and discontinuous employment" (Gill and Pratt 2008, 2). The proliferation of shows revolving around "real life" creative workers normalizes labor conditions that are spreading throughout the workforce as the extension of work, and the loss of control over work time, becomes the tradeoff for a cool job in a hot industry.

Talent competitions are a case in point. Competitions to become the next top model, celebrity chef or design star require contestants to work long hours of unpaid creative labor, all the while being monitored, evaluated, coached, judged and eliminated by experts. Being the most talented is never enough to win the prize: the successful contestants must demonstrate their resilience, flexibility and entrepreneurialism. It is telling that so many televised talent competitions are set in glamorized creative fields such as fashion, art, media, cuisine and design. As Angela McRobbie demonstrates in her study of fashion designers, the "talent-led economy" of self-expressive work demands "capacities for inexhaustible resourcefulness, resilience and entrepreneurialism" that set the stage for the future of postindustrial labor. However, even those who "maximize" their capacities for work are not guaranteed success, because these fields operate on a "lottery economy" in which the opportunities for success are limited (McRobbie 2002, 102). McRobbie argues that the rags-to-riches upward mobility fantasy has mutated into a more complex mediation of success and failure, in which seemingly random factors such as "bad timing" impact outcomes. This uncertainty is tolerated, she contends, because creative cultural work is presented as a "reward onto itself," a self-fulfilling enterprise.

This helps to explain why people take part in reality competitions like *MasterChef* and *Project Runway*. Participants who receive only small stipends for months of work serve as free labor for the TV industry. The risks are high, as there can be only one winner.

The possibility of pursing a reality TV gig as "its own reward" is tempered by the enterprising logic underscoring TV competitions. In her study of self-help career guides, Micki McGee (2005) notes that the artist and the entrepreneur are similar in that they both work "without any immediate sign of compensation." The desire for "unalienated labor, for engagement in one's work," drives both artists and entrepreneurs, despite their different motivation. This leads to two outcomes—"giving away the store (the artist's way) or working countless hours of overtime in order to 'brand' and 'market' one's self." On reality television, as in the postindustrial workforce at large, what were "once discreet categories—artist and entrepreneur— have collapsed," says McGee (2005, 136). The assumed payoff for free labor is the potential to capitalize on one's creativity and passion. When a belabored designer on *Project Runway* emerges from weeks of toil and wins a contract with a fashion company, or an eliminated contestant on *America's Next Top Model* (2003–2015) scores a magazine advertisement or a new reality show, reality television's potential to translate passion into profit is realized. Of course, as they put in hours of unpaid labor in the hopes of reaping future payoffs from the mantra of all work, all the time, reality participants are also producing economic value for the culture industries.

Here, the concept of *immaterial labor* is relevant. While early Marxists protested the labor exploitation inherent to the industrial production of tangible goods (such as automobiles or cans of soup), the postindustrial economy works differently. Profit hinges more on the commodification of feelings, images, attitudes, styles, identities, brands and expressions of social life. Newer "autonomist" Marxists emphasize the immaterial labor associated with a more expansive mode of capitalist production (Lazzarato 2006). For such scholars, the reign of the Fordist factory has given way to a "new epoch in which the factory is increasingly disseminated out into the society as a whole" (Gill and Pratt 2008, 6). Increasingly, we all perform degrees of immaterial labor. Our work is not limited to the work we perform for pay at the factory or the office: what we do and feel off the job can also be channeled into the "social factory," and used to generate profit for commercial industries, advertisers and postindustrial capitalism at large. From this vantage point, contestants on reality competitions do more than provide amateur talent for a cost-cutting TV industry. They also produce personas, fashions, associations and cultural meanings that feed in to the economic value for brands and television networks. When an aspiring top model rehearses a Cover Girl commercial as part of a weekly challenge, or a would-be top chef makes a meal out of ingredients provided by sponsors, their labor becomes part of the dispersed mode of capitalist production discussed by scholars. (When consumers post YouTube videos about their favorite Cover Girl products, or discuss *Top Chef* on Twitter, they are likewise engaging in immaterial labor to the extent that their social activity is channeled into the process of commodification and the economic value of industries and brands.)

The best example of immaterial labor in reality and lifestyle television is the TV show contest. On *The Next Food Network Star*, later called *Food Network Star* (2005–), contestants compete for the opportunity to host their own cooking show on the Food Network. Each week, they engage in challenges that test their cooking talents—as well as their personalities, camera readiness and charisma. The labor performed by participants ranges from working on

Team Giada

Figure 4.3 Contestants on *Food Network Star* are coached by the channel's brand name personalities.

and perfecting their appearances and people skills, to preparing food for the judges, to creating and adapting recipes, to producing entertainment value as amateur talent. This mix of affective, aesthetic and creative labor becomes immaterial when it produces value for the Food Network, which owns the rights to the dishes prepared for the show and the performances of the participants, and whose profitability as a cable network rests on its programming and brand image. Similarly, on *HGTV Star* (2006–2013) contestants compete to host an interior design program on the HGTV cable network. Each week they compete in challenges that range from redecorating rooms to showcasing products and brands to transforming entire homes for prizes like appearing in *HGTV Magazine* (which does not pay them for their designs). As with *Food Network Star*, there can be only one grand prize, and this encourages fierce competition and contingency plans. The staging of creative work in a meritocracy with enterprising undertones, which requires working for free similar to an unpaid intern, discourages any collective identification among worker-participants who may (or may not) be able to channel their experience into future rewards. Meanwhile, everything they create on the show is owned by HGTV, as are their images. Ordinary people seeking access to the TV industry as personalities and celebrity experts must tolerate uncertainty, risk, overwork and the commodification of their labor. Like the creative workers studied by McRobbie, most will be stymied by the "lottery economy" of reality television. As the host tells the losing contestants, "Your show has been cancelled . . . please exit the studio."

NOTE

1 My discussion of TV shows built around beauty service labor draws from my larger study, "Dream Jobs: The Glamorization of Beauty Service Labor in Media Culture," in *Aesthetic Labour: Rethinking Beauty Politics in Neoliberalism*, edited by Rosalind Gill, Christina Scharff and Ana Sophia Elias for Palgrave Macmillan. See Ouellette (2016) for a more comprehensive and theoretical analysis of this trend.

5

PERFORMING DIFFERENCE

In 2013, the TLC cable network launched a reality sitcom about the "crazy antics" of the residents of a trailer park in Myrtle Beach, South Carolina. *Trailer Park: Welcome to Myrtle Manor* (2013–) brings TV viewers inside the everyday lives of low-income people usually hidden from view, or stigmatized as debased and "trashy" when they do appear in the media. The prospect of an entire TV program revolving around the home life, relationships, occupations and leisure practices of trailer park residents promised unprecedented visibility—but many reviewers denounced the show for "ridiculing the underclass" by constructing caricatures of unintelligent, over-sexualized, alcohol and cigarette-addicted "trailer trash" for laughs. Commentators called into question the veracity of the program, noting that at least one lead character doesn't live at the trailer park and that producers spiced up the setting by adding an above-ground plastic swimming pool (perfect for skinny dipping) and a beauty shop (perfect for gossiping) that weren't there before the cameras arrived. The TV critic for *Variety* said the program seemed "inauthentic" and staged, noting that while "no writer is credited," the voiceover read by residents themselves comes across as a Hollywood version of "homespun" déclassé. The same critic also observed that the participants did not appear especially naïve or exploited, despite the cartoonish light in which they are portrayed. At a time when landing a gig on a reality show carries the promise of fame and fortune—at least in the popular imaginary—the residents of Myrtle Manor looked "eager to be in on the joke" (Lowry 2013).

Trailer Park: Welcome to Myrtle Manor is part of a burgeoning slice of reality entertainment revolving around the intimate lives, and lifestyles, of under-represented or marginalized groups (e.g. All-American Muslim, 2011–2012; Amish Mafia, 2012– ; Breaking Amish, 2012– ; Return to Amish, 2014– ; Breaking Amish: LA, 2015–), gypsies (My Big Fat Gypsy Wedding, 2012– ; American Gypsies, 2012; Gypsy Sisters, 2013–2015), people of small stature (Little People, Big World, 2006–2015; The Little Couple, 2009– ; Little Women: LA, 2014– ; Little Women: NY, 2015–), polygamous families (Sister Wives, 2010– ; My Five Wives, 2013–2014), and subcultures said to have "extreme" or abject lifestyles (Hoarding: Buried Alive, 2010–2013; My Strange Addiction, 2010– ; Extreme Cougar Wives, 2012). TLC is explicitly branded as a cable channel for program-ming about "different" people not usually afforded media representation. TLC's evolution as a cable channel mirrors the broader development of reality and lifestyle television in recent decades. The Learning Channel was founded in 1972 by the U.S. Department of Health, Education and Welfare and NASA as an "informative and instructional" network distributed free of charge via public satellite. Acquired by the Appalachian Community Service Network in 1980, the channel continued to air adult and children's edu-cational programs like Learn to Read (1987–2008), as well as documenta-ries about nature, history and science. In 1991, The Learning Channel was bought by Discovery Communications, Inc., a corporate media conglomer-ate which added more entertaining factual programs such as Trauma: Life in the ER (1997–2002), and how-to lifestyle programming such as home deco-rating and remodeling shows to the mix. In 1998, The Learning Channel was rebranded as simply TLC. The word learning was dropped, and real-ity entertainment revolving around unusual or exotic people and families (Acuna 2012) became its stock in trade.

Discovery describes TLC as the "only channel that uses real life storytell-ing to connect viewers to the breadth of the human experience through its 'life unscripted' approach." While this claim may be a stretch, TLC programming does present an alternative to the aspirational identities and opportunities for self-actualization emphasized by other lifestyle channels. Many TLC programs combine the conventions of comedy and soap opera with documentary-style treatments of people assumed to be outside mainstream society. The real-life participants on these shows are not pitched as figures to be emulated but as embodied markers of physical, ethnic, class and regional and other differences. While packaged as glossy entertainment, they rework TLC's association with education by allowing TV viewers to feel they are learning about the "wondrous difference" (Griffiths 2001) of individuals and subcultures they might not otherwise encounter. This nod to learning is partly rooted in the ethnographic documentary film tradition exemplified by Robert Flaherty's 1922 film *Nanook of the North*, which introduced moviegoers to the "exotic" ways of Indigenous Inuit people (as with much reality entertainment, scenes from Flaherty's film were staged for the camera). Having struck ratings gold with *Here Comes Honey Boo Boo* (2012–2014), a reality sitcom about the lives of a "redneck" family in rural Georgia spun off from *Toddlers and Tiaras* (2008–2013), an inside look at the Southern working-class world of child beauty pageants, TLC was eager for more popular programming that highlighted the cultural "difference" of the white working class. The motive for launching a show set in a trailer park was the realization that the spectacle of lower-class lifestyle can be a valuable commodity in an increasingly cluttered television marketplace.

While *Trailer Park: Welcome to Myrtle Manor* hinges on a claim to the real, it is cast, produced, filmed, edited and marketed as ratings-driven entertainment. Storylines are carefully crafted out of documentary-style footage in the model of the sitcom: "colorful" characters experience ordinary situations and problems in a hilarious manner. As with other reality shows, the participants are enlisted to "just be themselves, only more so," a directive that media sociologist Laura Grindstaff describes as a self-conscious performance of class (and other social differences) steeped in clichés circulating within the industry and society at large (2011a, 2014). While real people are clearly involved, they are enlisted to play loosely scripted "roles" designed to entertain audiences. The impetus for putting economically disadvantaged and socially marginalized people on television is what John Corner calls the high commodity value of "documentary as diversion" (2002). Whereas earlier forms of documentary were motivated by civic aims such as public education and social critique, documentary as diversion is driven by commercial ambitions. While TLC programs are often

Figure 5.1 Subtitles on Trailer Park: Welcome to Myrtle Manor position the cast as outside of U.S. society.

rationalized as educational in the sense of early anthropological films about unusual or exoticized others, they are conceived as moneymaking cultural products, and any new opportunities for diversifying representation they provide are constrained by this commercially driven framework.

TLC is not alone in recognizing the commodity value of "real" difference. Today, a large segment of reality entertainment brings visibility to individuals and subcultures heretofore marginalized on television, from people of Iranian descent (Shahs of Sunset, 2012–) to Italian American "guidos" and "guidettes" (Jersey Shore, 2009–2012) to rural alligator hunters in the swamp region of Louisiana (Swamp People, 2010–) to young women living with paralysis in Hollywood (Push Girls, 2012–2013). Many of these reality productions have been charged with embellishing the truth for entertainment value, and downplaying the political dimensions of difference and the inequalities upon which it often rests. Still, there is no denying that reality entertainment has greatly expanded social representation on television, and that some reality TV participants have become celebrities who actively participate in their constitution as TV characters. This chapter analyzes the performance of difference across reality and lifestyle programming, and situates the focus on marginalized and underrepresented groups within broader debates about the influx of ordinary people in the media, the role of performance in identity and reality TV production, and the circulation of race, class and other social differences as commodities, lifestyles and brands.

FREAK SHOW: ORDINARY BUT DIFFERENT

In *Freak Show: First Person Media and Factual Television* (2000), Jon Dovey traces the origins of reality programs like *Trailer Park: Welcome to Myrtle Manor* to the 1990s. His analysis of talk shows, amateur video programs, video diaries, docusoaps and other early reality programs revolving around the private experiences of ordinary people identified trends that have continued to intensify. While the term *freak show* has historically evoked a "pejorative" view of sideshow circus entertainment, television formats that fused actuality and entertainment were mainstreaming the concept and making the freak show our "new public space," Dovey argued. The new reality formats were opening up new spaces for expressing identity, and performing and displaying difference. Suddenly, he observed, television was bursting with a wide range of ordinary people "proclaiming their own 'freakishness', articulating their most intimate fears and secrets, performing the ordinariness of their own extraordinary subjectivity" (2000, 4). This wasn't happening in news or documentary but in popular factual entertainment. Boundaries between fact and fiction were blurring as "tidal waves of entertainment" flooded into "discursive zones previously reserved for education, information and enlightenment," and real people performed their identities and differences within a popular "theater of intimacy." Dovey called the new formats *first person media* because they seemed to value "raw intimate experience" and "self-spoken narratives of everyday life" over objective knowledge or coherent narratives for making sense of the world (2000, 25–26). Even traditional documentary programs were impacted, Dovey claimed, as the documentary mode as a whole "increasingly concerned itself with the subject's inner life, the individual feelings of ordinary folk in any everyday situation with dramatic potential" (2000, 109).

To be sure, there are precursors to the "subjective, autobiographical and confessional modes of expression" (Dovey 2000, 2) associated with what we now call reality television. For example, the popular magazine

True Story, which inspired radio and television programs, circulated "first hand" accounts of personal tragedy, deviance and redemption as early as the 1930s (Mandziuk 2001). However, the mainstreaming of these modes of expression is linked to intersecting developments that have accelerated since the 1990s, including the deregulation of broadcasting, the waning of the public interest tradition, the growth of niche channels, industry cost-cutting strategies, the proliferation of new media technologies (such as portable video cameras), the rising concern with the self as a reflexive project, and the "posting" of social movements (such as feminism and civil rights), which are assumed to have already completed their missions. In most cases, the invitation for ordinary people to participate in television does not arise from efforts to democratize or diversify media, but from these wider developments and pressures. What worried Dovey was that real people were being recruited to share the intimate details of their daily existence in an industrial context that offered little control to its subjects. The problem was not the demise of documentary as a "discourse of sobriety" at the hands of popular entertainment (Nichols 1994), but the constraints faced by the "speaking subject within the frame of somebody else's version of their biographical narrative" (Dovey 2000, 110). These constraints have only been magnified as the TV industry has continued to develop reality formats (such as reality sitcoms) that enlist ordinary people to perform versions of themselves for ratings.

As Graeme Turner argues, ordinary people (defined as non-actors) have become even more visible since the 1990s as they are turned into media content via many platforms, from talk radio to blogs. Reality television, he observes, has been the "most extensive mechanism for this renewed interest in the ordinary, with its omnivorous appetite for new 'talent' and its extraordinary appeal for those wishing to make the transition from being an ordinary person to a media person" (2014, 310). Indeed, ordinary people have become integral to a business model that values free (or cheap) talent, and flexible and "speeded up" production cycles. Unlike earlier forms of stardom, the new forms of "ordinary celebrity" associated with reality television are disposable by design, Turner contends, manufactured by the TV industry and tossed aside once their economic value has been extracted (Turner 2006, 2010).

While it may seem as if television is now bursting with ordinary people "speaking for themselves," they are following the roles, conventions and "scripts" that popular reality formats require of them. All factual television, from documentaries to the gritty images of true crime programs, is mediated—reality is never captured "in the raw." The question is not whether production choices shape the reality presented to TV viewers, but *how* this is done and *toward what ends*. Vicki Mayer argues that the process begins with casting: the participants of reality shows are cast according to commercial objectives that set the stage for their "authentic" performances. Reality programs employ professional casters who package and sell "flattened types of characters" to producers, says Mayer. Her ethnographic research shows that casters search not only for people with certain demographics, but specifically for people who embody the *assumed traits of those demographics* (2011, 189). Successful casting involves targeting the "ideal cast member for a specific production, a process that converts the real person into an objectified type," says Mayer. In 2009, when Mayer was conducting her research on casting agents, the typology of characters in reality television drew from "familiar clichés about identity," and included such "archetypes as the white, male geek; the blond nemesis; and the soccer mom; as well as new but prominent token figures such as the gay assistant, the black sidekick, and the disabled or South Asian woman." In the new economy of television production, the "ideal reality cast member fits a type while displaying enough difference to make the type new and fresh," she contends (2014, 61).

Mayer's findings on the "reliance on types," and the need for race, class and disability as commodified markers of difference, suggests that the "pigeonholing and stereotyping many scholars see in reality television narratives may originate in the caster's corner" (2014, 62). The surge of reality entertainment about working-class Southern "rednecks" exemplifies this pigeonholing process, as the success of one show leads to the cementing of a marketable "type" that becomes part of the caster's repertoire. So, too, does the appearance of multiple programs about Amish people, polygamous families, little people and other "unusual" people, with each show providing a slight new twist on a social identity packaged and sold in the language of clichés. As Robert McRuer points out, *The Littlest Groom* (2004)—the first reality program to cast people of small stature—was conceived as an exotic variation on the dating format. Set in a luxurious mansion, the program followed a "short-statured man selecting his date" from a group of "beautiful short-statured women" who competed for a two-carat diamond ring and a romantic Mediterranean cruise with the bachelor of their dreams (2006, 58). *The Littlest Groom* connected the established conventions and character types—which are already based on gender and class stereotypes—to a spectacle of physical difference. TV viewers were invited to "step right up to the circus that is Fox television" (2006, 58) while taking comfort in the reproduction of norms and conventions (wealth, the heterosexual family) familiar from other reality shows. While alternative readings were certainly possible, the impetus for staging *The Littlest Groom* was to sell the Other to mainstream audiences.

Othering is the process of creating and policing imaginary boundaries between "us" and "them." It is a power dynamic in which marginalized groups are constituted as different from or inferior to the imagined center of society. Edward Said identified techniques of othering in his work on colonialism (1979), and the concept has been adapted to critically analyze media's treatment of race, ethnicity, sexual orientation, geopolitics and disability. In her essay "Eating the Other," bell hooks (1992) argues that Otherness is often commodified by the media for the pleasure of mainstream audiences. "Ethnicity becomes a spice," she argues, a "seasoning that can liven up the dull dash that is mainstream white culture" (1992, 21). When one or two people of color are included in an otherwise white reality show, or U.S. productions like *America's Next Top Model* or *The Amazing Race* visit a non-Western country, racial and ethnic difference may be offered up as a "dash of spice" that adds entertainment (and commercial value). Programs that invite TV viewers imagined as the center of society to peer into the everyday lives of underrepresented and marginalized groups also deploy Othering tactics. The proliferation of shows about small people since *The Littlest Groom* is one example.

These programs cast their subjects as people who are "just like us," but spectacularly different. *The Little Couple* (2009–) follows the lives of an ordinary couple followed by cameras because they are small. TV viewers are invited to observe as they have children, work, become romantic and live a scripted version of their lives on screen. The program demonstrates that people with physical differences can pursue so-called "normal" lives—and in this sense, it may partly unravel stereotypes and question the imaginary boundaries between "us" and "them." At the same time, the show trades on voyeurism and is pitched to an audience imagined to occupy the unmarked center from which difference is identified and normalized. *The Little Couple* is not designed to offer meaningful representations for those who share the social experience of the cast, but to sell up close and personal encounters with difference to the consuming audience. Tellingly, there is no attention to historical and ongoing struggles over public policies to ensure the accommodation and equal treatment of people with physical differences.

Occasionally, information about the medical condition of dwarfism is offered online, but this material is distanced from the storylines and buried amidst teasers, bonus scenes and episode recaps. The website for *Little People, Big World*, a program about a mixed-size relationship, links to a page of "frequently asked questions" and answers about dwarfism, and reminds TV viewers that people of small stature should not be called by the offensive label "midgets." As with the show itself, this attempt at public education is geared to an imaginary "us" and is stripped of any broader struggle over rights and resources. When identity politics is addressed, it is often subsumed by an appeal to drama or comedy. In the trailer for the debut of *Little Women: LA* (2014–), a docusoap about a friend group obsessed with dating and shopping in the vein of the *Real Housewives* franchise, participants express their anger at pejorative terms like "midget" and "handicap," and demand to be treated as full members of society. However, this brief scene quickly segues into many more scenes in which the women yell, gossip about one another, slam doors and fight over men, setting the stage for the emotional conflict and drama that TV viewers are promised.

Once a reality program has been cast, other production choices shape and constrain the intimate participation of ordinary people. Setting, narrative conventions, editing, lighting and wardrobe decisions convey the producers' vision of people who appear as themselves on screen. Behind-the-scenes coaching and confessional interviews designed to magnify drama and build characters are impactful as well. These mediating strategies also convey to TV viewers whether the cast members are to be admired or ridiculed, identified with or consumed from afar. For example, the consistent use of subtitles in shows like *Here Comes Honey Boo Boo* positions lower-class whites (particularly in the South) outside the boundaries of mainstream America due to their inability to command proper English. These programs bring more visibility to working-class cultures historically marginalized by U.S. television, but they ignore economic inequality and code class difference as a voluntary matter of lifestyle and taste through closeups on missing teeth and fleshy bodies, and storylines "mapped out in advance" (Corner 2002, 256) involving junk food, road kill, tractor pulls, mud wrestling contests and other stereotypical props and settings deployed in humorous ways, to convey social inferiority. The depiction of "white trash" on shows like *Trailer Park: Welcome to Myrtle Manor* works in a similar way. As Laura Grindstaff points out, the term white trash is a racial qualifier that names whiteness only when poor white people are assumed to violate the dominant codes of whiteness by acting "trashy" (2011a, 200). The concept presumes a racial hierarchy and identifies some white people as an exception, hence the need to qualify their whiteness. On *Myrtle Manor*, trashiness is signified through subtitles, close-ups of roach-infested trailer homes, muscle cars and scenes staged for the camera in which beer-drinking park residents bash old TV sets in their front yards for fun. While the show has a jokey air about it, exemplified by episode titles like "Days of Our Lives Trailer Park" and "My Big Fat Trailer Park Wedding," this only makes it easier to construct a hierarchy between "us" and the real people depicted on screen. Any "raw intimate experience" about trailer park life is constrained by production decisions and the clichés upon which they rest.

Reality shows revolving around gypsies operate in a similar vein. A cluster of shows about the descendants of Roma people and Travellers, the ethnic groups "lumped together under the term 'gypsy'," have proliferated in the United Kingdom as well as the United States. *American Gypsies, Big Fat Gypsy Weddings, My Big Fat American Gypsy Wedding, Gypsy Sisters* and other shows erase a history of political disenfranchisement (including enslavement, segregation, deportation to concentration camps during World War II, chronic poverty and forced migration) and play up stereotypes of nomads with bizarre traditions and gaudy tastes. As Mona Nicoară (2012) points out, these programs are "invested in reproducing a version of what it means to be a 'gypsy' that broadcasters believe to be most comfortable for their audience—Esmeralda-like headscarves, belly dancing, innate violence, gaudy parties, psychic healing parlors." They also imply that the communities featured on the shows have happily chosen to live "on the edge of society," by stressing their exotic traditions. *American Gypsies* begins by telling TV viewers "For over 1,000 years, Romany or Gypsy people have remained hidden from view—until now," writes Nicoară, while the UK's *Big Fat Gypsy Weddings* was announced with the slogan "Bigger. Fatter. Gypsier."

The U.S. version of *My Big Fat Gypsy Wedding* promises to help Roma people tell their stories so the "rest of the world can understand and appreciate their culture" and let TV viewers "take a peek at their contemporary lives." However, the show's participants do not speak for themselves, as much as they perform Otherness for the pleasure of the audience. Cast as unrefined, garish, loud, overly emotional, violent and trashy, their difference is marked by many of the attributes assigned to trailer park residents and low-income class cultures. The audience is not expected to identify with the characters, but to enjoy their difference from afar, partly as a means of assuring their own superiority. On the show's website, viewers learn "10 Ways to Go Gypsy at Your Wedding," but are not expected to follow the advice on offer. The copy reinforces a hierarchy between "us" and "them" by poking fun at the flamboyant and "excessive" costumes and traditions presented on the TV program, and telling readers: "Beauty isn't in the eyes of the beholder. There's a pretty standard formula every woman can follow to get gypsy gorgeous. Get thee to a spray tanning salon. Whiten your teeth. And have a manicurist add the longest, most brightly colored acrylics imaginable to your fingertips. You're halfway there! Now, you just need a few hair extensions, a generous dusting of body glitter and a swipe of pretty pink lipstick. You're ready for the altar (and you're welcome)."

When real people (including the participants on *American Gypsies*) are invited to appear on television, their performances are cued to the demands of commercial entertainment. As John Corner observes (2002), participants of reality programs are induced to "perform the real" within formulas and conventions, even as the shows trade on the assumption that the camera captures authentic behavior. We have all been trained in the tropes and stock characters of docusoaps, gamedocs and reality sitcoms, and people who appear on these shows are no exception. According to Laura Grindstaff, producers reinforce these expectations in the service of drama and cost

Figure 5.2 *My Big Fat American Gypsy Wedding* presents Roma people as exotic Others for mainstream consumption.

efficiency. Producers do not impose scripts as much as they construct the "conditions of possibility for specific performances out of particular narrative contexts so that participants can serve themselves, cafeteria style, to ready made roles without the bother of extensive training, scripts, rehearsals or even talent" (2011a, 205). Ironically, says Grindstaff, the presumed authenticity of a character or storyline "does not preclude the performance of cultural clichés," but indeed seems to demand recognizable templates that are easy to perform without "explicit scripting or rehearsal" (Grindstaff 2009, 81). One way that authenticity is registered (and commodified) is through what Grindstaff calls the "money shot," or the heightened moment where ordinary people become angry or sad and lose control over their performance. Beverly Skeggs and Helen Wood call the corollary use of production practices like editing or "ironic voiceover" to undermine the agency of the ordinary subject, the "judgment shot" (2011, 16). For example, in the debut episode of *Here Comes Honey Boo Boo*, the family matriarch tells the camera that while she may not be "beautimous" she's pretty good looking. The program questions her assessment of herself—and encourages the TV viewer to regard the character as physically abject—by zooming in on her double chins and inserting an awkward pause when she is finished talking.

TV viewers are not unaware of the crafted dimensions of reality story-telling: while reality programming is differentiated in the marketplace by a difference from fiction, the evocation of realism is increasingly playful, and "belief in the veracity of what you are watching is not a prerequisite to engagement and pleasure" (Corner 2002, 45). While reality programs are sometimes accused of incidents of fakery, and participants are called out for playing to the camera, these concerns tend to conceal the "performance logic" of *all* reality programming. Instead of asking if shows like *Trailer Park: Welcome to Myrtle Manor* are sufficiently "real," we might ask how identity and difference are performed on the shows, and for what purposes. As Grindstaff points out, the performative logic of reality television is not entirely the result of industry practices but is also culturally consistent with the "seepage of performance demands into everyday life," and a growing incitement to externalize the self—to watch others "play themselves" and be "watched in return" (2011a, 201). Reality television participants are "performing performance" in that they "dramatize how we all project and perform in real life" (Grindstaff 2014, 314). They "make conscious the usually unconscious, habitual performances of everyday," and in that sense may model a broader "turn toward performativity in numerous occupational, political and cultural fields" (Deery 2015, 31). While everyone from coffee shop baristas to politicians is called upon to perform as a condition of their jobs, performativity also unfolds in the intimate spaces of everyday life. Social theorists have come to understand identity as performative (Butler 1990), in the sense of "unconscious repeated gendered and class enactments" that can, in some circumstances, become "full-blown conscious actions" (Skeggs and Wood 2011, 17). When reality participants are called upon to "be themselves, only more so," taken-for-granted and unconscious "enactments of social difference can be made into conscious deliberations and acts as they are called into a . . . televised performance" (2011, 17).

Gender is especially theorized as performative: what we think of as masculinity and femininity are not innate or biological differences, but rather "stylized repetition of acts" that are "always a reiteration of a norm or set of norms," which means that the "act that one does, the act that one performs is, in a sense, an act that has been going on before one arrived at the scene" (Diamond 1996, 4–6, cited in Madison and Hamera 2005, xviii). Julie

Bettie points out that other differences, such as class, can also be conceptualized as performative in that "there is no [innate or] interior difference that is being expressed; rather, institutionalized class inequality creates class subjects who perform, or display, differences in cultural capital" (Bettie 2000, 11, cited in Grindstaff 2011a, 199). Reality television incites exaggerated performances of working-class identity. This has contradictory implications, as it de-emphasizes the material basis of inequalities while also potentially exposing the unstable and socially determined nature of class and other identities. While "cultural capital" is lived and felt at the level of social space and the body, it can also be a mobile "set of aesthetic qualities and moral/behavioral dispositions that can be enacted by and attributed to different groups regardless of material circumstance" (Grindstaff 2011a, 200). This means that people can perform class status, regardless of their economic position. The performance of white trash—a racial qualifier that names whiteness only when white people violate the dominant codes of whiteness by acting "trashy"—is a case in point. According to Grindstaff, white trash (or trailer trash) can be performed as a "television persona by virtually anyone willing to adopt its codes," regardless of whether or not they are actually "poor, white, and/or living in a trailer park," she contends. Shows like Jerry Springer and Jersey Shore, she claims, are like modern minstrelsy, with participants eager to appear on television for a variety of reasons "performing in trash face" (2011a, 200).

The "excessive" class coding of Jersey Shore (2009–2012), a show where eight self-described guidos and guidettes ("not all of Italian descent" and only one of whom actually comes from the Shore) live and party together in a New Jersey resort town, exaggerates class markers associated with white working-class Italian Americans. The cast members are cast as "trashy" through their regional accents, unsophisticated tastes (one participant arrives at the set with her belongings stuffed in black trash bags in lieu of a suitcase), stupidity, lack of ambition and unrefined bodily excesses. They are filmed living in the future tense, seeking immediate gratifications and unrefined bodily pleasures—the more the better. These are stereotypes of the lower classes, embodied to excess by the youthful Jersey Shore cast by "having a lot of sex and showing a lot of skin, usually after consuming vast quantities of alcohol" (Grindstaff 2011a, 199). While this potentially reveals class as an "act" rather than an inborn or innate identity, it still perpetuates class hierarchies and conveys the idea that differences in cultural capital (aesthetic tastes, bodily comportment, manners) are the "choices of individual subjects who could presumably act differently if they chose" (2011a, 202). The extent to which the participants of *Jersey Shore* have capitalized on their television exposure to launch merchandise lines and personal brands conceals the economic dimensions of class and the power of the TV industry to dictate and control the terms by which ordinary people can participate in the media.

Working-class cultural capital has historically had little exchange value, meaning that it cannot be traded for things like income or social status. Reality television creates highly publicized exceptions to this rule. Successful shows like *Jersey Shore* and *Here Comes Honey Boo Boo* promise to catapult cast members into disposable celebrities who can capitalize on the performance of working-class cultural codes, however ridiculed or stereotyped. Participants often promote themselves through social media, and some have become mainstays in the tabloids and on talk shows and comedy circuits. While this attention is often negative—the cast of *Honey Boo Boo* was regularly parodied and mocked by everyone from David Letterman to *Saturday Night Live* during its heyday—it constitutes a type of ordinary celebrity that is assumed to have market value. The cast of *Duck Dynasty* (2012–), a show about a backwoods Louisiana family that became wealthy selling duck calls, has spawned a thriving line of merchandise including "shirts, caps, coolers, books, edibles and hunting gear of every kind." Envisioned by the A&E network as a "real life" cross between *The Waltons* and *The Beverly Hillbillies*, *Duck Dynasty* airs in more than one hundred countries and was dubbed the "biggest reality show in the history of cable" by the *New York Times* (Carter 2013). Likewise, the participants of *Sister Wives*, a formerly low-income polygamous family that once filed for bankruptcy and received government aid, have use their TV program to "promote their family arrangement as a part of a growing wave of individual lifestyle choices," and turned their "cause into a minor industry" that includes a bestselling book, four new houses and a "personal brand" (Schwartz 2014). While the vast majority of people who appear on reality shows become neither rich nor famous, the specter of transforming ordinariness—and the spectacle of difference—into personal fame and fortune looms large, perpetuated by examples like these.

THE PROLIFERATION OF DIFFERENCE

Peep-show entertainment invites TV viewers to revel in the intimate lives of Others who perform authentic difference within commercially driven entertainment frameworks. While lip service is sometimes paid to educating the public about difference, the emphasis is on transforming "private lives into public spectacle through an emphasis on drama and performance over information" (Wood and Skeggs 2011, 6). The rise of documentary as diversion has required hybrid entertainment formats that rouse the emotions but rarely contextualize or critique power dynamics. While popular fictional genres like soap operas, sitcoms and dramas have addressed social issues and political tensions, reality entertainment has rarely done so. Instead, much programming conveys the assumption that the United States is now a multicultural society where social identities are increasingly fluid, and discrimination based on class, ethnicity, ability and race no longer takes place. The incitement to self-actualization, self-transformation and self-enterprising across reality and lifestyle formats encourages private solutions to lingering inequalities and problems. Within a market-oriented neoliberal context, differences of race and ethnicity are shorn from a history of political struggle and recast in the language of "already achieved" equality, consumption and individual choice.

Catherine Squires argues that, like the dominant media in general, reality and lifestyle television assumes that the civil rights movement has accomplished its goals and that no further government action or social activism is required to achieve racial equality. This postracial sensibility, she points out, draws on the "neoliberal assumptions of market individualism" discussed in earlier chapters, "where race/ethnicity present us with specific kinds of choices to be negotiated: whether to display or not display racial identities, whether to consume or not consume the cultural products of other groups" (2014, 264). The idea that race is a commodity that can be strategically performed and capitalized on by individuals is part of this logic as well. Squires and other scholars point to *America's Next Top Model*, a competition for aspiring models competing for a cash prize and a contract with Cover Girl, as an example. Hosted by famed African American supermodel and entrepreneur Tyra Banks, *Top Model* assembles a diverse cast each "cycle" with many women of color, many of whom are lower-income. While this constructs an image of a multicultural society in which everyone can compete for equality of opportunity, critics argue that the market logic underpinning the show only validates performances of race/ethnicity that are deemed "saleable." *Top Model* acknowledges that racial identity (like gender and class) is not inborn or fixed but culturally determined and fluid. This understanding is fused to the incitement to strategically perform race/ethnicity in particular ways that are deemed to have market value. Contestants of color are coached to "work" their race/ethnicity—to "embrace the particular aspects of their non-white racialization that the market deems attractive" and hide the rest (Hasinoff 2008, 340, cited in Squires 2014, 266). Racial flexibility is prized as a competitive advantage that allows some contestants to "provide the modeling industry with an array of 'looks' that are salable in a time of multiracial chic" (Hasinoff 2008, 335, cited in Squires 2014, 266). As Squires points out, not all racial looks are valued within this system. The idea that race can be performed for commercial reward is steeped in regional and class hierarchies, as is revealed when lower-income black women from the South are continually advised to lose their accents to make themselves more marketable (2014, 266).

As Ralina Joseph argues, Tyra Banks embodies the market advantages of being able to "constantly shift racialized codes" (2012, 125). She "performs" as "particularly African American, or desirable to a niche market, and universally post-racial, or accessible to all racialized audiences" (2012, 128). Following Banks' "celebrity commodity lead," *Top Model* conveys the message that winning the competition—and succeeding in life—requires being able to transform one's mannerisms, speech and looks to "appear post-racial." In her analysis of a 2005 episode in which the contestants must "switch races" for a Got Milk campaign, Joseph argues that treating race as a "make up effect" disavows the realities of structural racism (2012, 129). While *Top Model* conveys the idea that race can be tried on and "sloughed off at will" (2012, 153), like many reality programs it still "relies on authentic signifiers" of difference rooted in racialized stereotypes. "Race is real in that it is something that is visually and sometimes orally signified and it comes with specific commodities, for example so-called racially appropriate hair, nails and makeup. However, race is also constructed so that such

significations can be switched through performance and commodities,"
Joseph explains (2012, 144). What Joseph calls a "racialized masquerade"
invites TV viewers of all racialized identities to witness a market-driven process of "race transcendence" that conceals the "real effects" of institutionalized racism, poverty and the bodily markers of race (2012, 148).

As Squires points out, "ethnic/racial difference in the marketplace is a
necessary element of postracial approaches to culture and consumption."

Figure 5.3 Contestants on *America's Next Top Model* "switch" races for a Got Milk
advertising campaign.

The postracial logic of reality and lifestyle television is not "colorblind," but rather racial and ethnic identities are presented as niche lifestyles and consumer preferences operating at a distance from the "facts of racism" (2014, 267). This is not surprising to the extent that affirmative action programs to ensure diversity in the workplace (including television production) are on the wane and public interest mandates such as the Fairness Doctrine, which required broadcasters to provide "equal time" to diverse perspectives, have been dismantled (Amaya 2010; Perlman 2012). Today, racial diversity in television culture is left entirely to the hands of the free market, which means that commercial objectives dictate the casting and performance of people of color in all programming, including reality and lifestyle entertainment. While people of color sometimes appear as subjects in how-to lifestyle programming, there are remarkably few lifestyle experts of color—home decorators, makeover gurus, chefs—on broadcast or cable channels. As we saw in earlier chapters, the promotion of self-transformation as a path to security and success, which has become so prevalent in postindustrial societies with diminished public services, is rooted in the dissemination of white, educated, upper middle-class expertise. When lower-income people of color are "made over," white bourgeoisie norms are presented to them as a means of entry to the middle class. On shows like From G's to Gents (2008–2009), this provides the basis for much comedy as lower-income male "gangsters" are ultimately unable to pass themselves off as so-called gentlemen by donning prep school wardrobes, learning elite manners and etiquette, and mastering cricket and other white aristocratic sports. While the makeover logic of From G's to Gents is over the top, it still conveys the idea that performing racial and class fluidity is crucial to individual success in a neoliberal economy, and those who fail to transform themselves—or at least pass as "gentlemen"— have no one to blame but themselves. At the same time, the racialized underclass is commodified to provide stereotypical signifiers of "authenticity." Like the black and brown subjects of COPS (1989–) and other programs about the policing of mainly poor neighborhoods of color, the classed racialized "G's" are rendered visible not for civic purposes or as an incitement to political activism, but as the raw material for reality entertainment (Ouellette 2011).

The message that poor people of color "choose" their situations is complemented by the proliferation of reality programs about wealthy African

American celebrities and social circles. As Squires points out, these "domestic consumerist docudramas" partly mirror the casting and storytelling conventions of all-white reality programs, but substitute black characters (2014, 268). For example, *Real Housewives of Atlanta* (2008–) is the only program in the multiseries franchise about the emotional dramas and consumption practices of wealthy women to feature African American women as main characters. This racial segregation, Squires contends, is recast by postracial logic as "just another choice on a menu of possible ways to express one's lifestyle preferences" (2014, 268). Reality programs that draw inspiration from *Keeping Up With the Kardashians* (2007) to highlight the personal lives and lavish lifestyles of people of color add "multicultural spice" to the upscale docusoap, and invite TV viewers to be voyeurs in "communities they may never enter in real life," Squires contends. (2014, 272). Shows like *Basketball Wives* (2011–) and the *Love & Hip Hop* franchise (2010–) reinforce the assumption of a postracial society by constructing race as a lifestyle and a consumer choice with little relationship to structural conditions of racism and class oppression, says Squires.

The *Love & Hip Hop* franchise is a multiseries docusoap about "striving for stardom in the rap game while trying to survive relationship and family struggles." *Love & Hip Hop: New York* (2010–), *Love & Hip Hop: Atlanta* (2012–) and *Love & Hip Hop: Hollywood* (2014–) feature mainly African American casts and are geared to black audiences as well as white ones. The characters are not cast as pathologized or exoticized Others in the vein of small people, "white trash" or gypsies, but as embodiments of a lavish hip hop lifestyle. As with much reality and lifestyle television, the differentiation and performance of racial identity is linked to the aestheticization of everyday life through lavish displays of wealth that "reinforce the postracial, neoliberal argument that the market now provides all individuals access to equal opportunity" (Squires 2014, 275). At the same time, racial identity is enacted through codes of "ghetto fabulousness," and "black conspicuous consumption" is depicted as an "excessive and out of control striving for bling" (2014, 275; see also Mukherjee 2011). VH1 plays up these mixed messages, simultaneously casting the participants as aspirational figures and problematizing their excessive tastes. The cable network promoted the cast reunion for *Love & Hip Hop: Hollywood* with photographs of the participants "showing off their bling." Close-ups of necklaces, rings and jewels signify wealth and success, but are framed by the message: "Coco Chanel's famous saying 'Before you leave the house, take a look in the mirror and take one thing off' may not quite apply to the cast of *Love & Hip Hop: Hollywood*." Ultimately, performing oneself "only more so" on reality television may be more complicated for people of color forced to navigate the convergence of postracial ideology and market logic. Squires cites the example of a *Top Model* contestant who was praised for her "ghetto fab" style one minute but later reprimanded for "not tempering that style . . . celebrated as authentic and keeping it real one moment and accused of squandering" her chances for success at another (2014, 275).

The paradox of racial performance in reality television speaks to the shifting politics of representation since the 1990s. As Sarah Banet-Weiser argues (2007b), the forms of empowerment associated with media visibility have become disassociated from social movements and reformulated as market strategies (2007b, 213). Representations of people of color have proliferated, and race is now used to signify hip urban flair as well as criminality, but this has not been accompanied by "changes in poverty levels, unemployment, policy and education" (2007b, 214). Indeed, Herman Gray identifies a "waning" of what a politics of representation can yield as race and other differences are aligned with conceptions of the "self-crafting entrepreneurial subject," who must fend for herself in new practices of government and whose diversity only matters as a "commodity or source of brand value" (2013, 771). Gray points out that the State has been the primary site of "struggles for social recognition and social equality" through civil rights, equality of opportunity and affirmative action policies. As these gains have been downsized and jettisoned, media continued to operate as a "crucial site where different sectors of disenfranchised populations and communities continue to seek (and in some cases have achieved) recognition and greater visibility." Because the proliferation of difference in the cultural realm no longer correlates with collective grievances in the political sphere, the gains of media visibility remain uncertain, Gray contends.

While "differences of all sorts—racial, gender, sexual, regional, religious, body type, and so on—abound and proliferate in media spaces," from reality television to social media platforms like Facebook, the quest for visibility seems to have become "the end itself," says Gray (2013, 772). While social media activism around police shootings of people of color and the rise of the Black Lives Matter movement complicate this analysis, Gray's point is that visibility has proliferated in a market-based society where racial difference is for sale. When public welfare is privatized, and the terms of "belonging, narrating the self and performing identity and difference" are colonized by consumer culture and branding (2013, 777), media become fraught as a site of social change. We can no longer assume, Gray contends, that correcting inaccuracies or demanding more images of under-represented and marginalized groups has any correspondence to "collective claims on the State" (2013, 778). Certainly, the TV industry's embracing of race as a commodity, and the parallel incitement for participants to perform race/ethnicity in the service of launching careers, building brands and crafting marketable personas, renders reality television more complicit than not with postracial hegemony.

GIVING AN ACCOUNT OF ONESELF

In *Why Voice Matters: Culture and Politics After Neoliberalism* (2010), Nick Couldry describes this dilemma as a "crisis of voice" in contemporary times. While social media, reality television and other mediated forums for ordinary people to speak have proliferated dramatically, these venues for "speaking the self" are dominated by logics of self-enterprise, privatization and consumption. Couldry cites YouTube videos as an example of an "expanded zone of self-display," which epitomizes neoliberalism's impetus to commodify the human, to the extent that "page views and positive commentary on people's postings of themselves performing or simply 'being themselves' can literally be counted and monetized as part of the process of self-branding" (2010, 82). While there is no formal or mandatory "script," YouTubers often write themselves into a narrative that is "not theirs to adapt or control," and that represents a "deep denial of voice, a deep form of oppression," Couldry contends (2010, 9). Reality television pre-dated and arguably shaped social media platforms like YouTube as a site in which ordinary people are invited to perform marketable (and often stereotypical) versions of themselves in the hopes of monetizing their personas and brands (Hearn 2010).

Couldry advocates an expansion of "voice that matters" as an alternative to neoliberal narratives of personhood. Voice, for him, is more than an expression of opinion or a claim to representation (in the media or the political system): voice is the "process of giving an account of one's life and its conditions," he contends. To have a voice entails an open-ended engagement with oneself, a process of reflecting "back and forth" between one's actions and experiences, and also relies on narrative, a "basic feature of human action" (2010, 7, 9). Giving an account of oneself involves telling a story about oneself and the social world in which one acts. This is not the same as fashioning identity and lifestyle through consumption and marketable performances of the self, but it does have affinities to the development of an "ethical relationship with the self" discussed in earlier chapters.

For Couldry, voice is urgently needed not as a way to achieve the "good life," or even a beautiful life in the ethical sense, but as a way to challenge the priorities and widening inequalities of neoliberal societies. Couldry attributes the crisis of voice to the unequal distribution of resources for having a voice that is "recognized and validated," and the widening "gap between people's lives and the narratives available" to define them in societies where individuals are called upon to adopt norms and behaviors drawn from the logic of the market, such as competition, self-branding and self-enterprising. The gap between dominant templates for selfhood and the articulation of lived experience matters, for to "deny value to another's capacity for narrative—deny her potential for voice—is to deny a basic dimension of human life," he contends (2010, 7).

This conception of voice is helpful for making sense of reality television, its relationship to ordinary people, and its enlistment of marginalized and underrepresented groups. Voice moves us beyond questions about the accuracy (or not) of claims to the real, to a more complex understanding of how subjective experience can be communicated, and the implications of this process. Voice is not guaranteed by references to intimacy, interiority or ordinariness. Placing a camera on a real person, setting up a confessional booth or authorizing someone to "be themselves, only more so" on television do not in themselves constitute voice. Drawing from Judith Butler (2005), Couldry theorizes voice as an "embodied process" of articulating the world that will draw from a history of reflection and self-interpretation.

Voice can be expressed in personal or collective ways, but it never arises from individuals in isolation, because "having a voice" is a social process, requiring the shared resources integral to recognition, interpretation and validation. Voice is not a "true" expression of a pre-constituted or authentic self, but is part of the ongoing project of selfhood.

Indeed, voice is not expressed as much as it is always performed. Butler's view of "authenticity" as a process of performance parallels discussions about the cultural basis of identity and the self-conscious performance of class, race and other social differences in reality television. She adds to this conversation the possibility of challenging, as well as perpetuating norms, despite reality television's overarching tendency to marketize social difference. "The 'I' has no story of its own that is not also the story of a relation— or set of relations—to a set of norms," Butler argues (2005, 8). There is no authentic personhood outside the norms and conventions of society—"self-making" outside the norms that "orchestrate the possible forms that a subject may take" is impossible. But this does not mean that voice is impossible. Butler argues that the use of voice as a critical social process must expose the limits of what is taken for granted. To narrate the self and its conditions in this way is to maintain a "critical relation" to existing norms, Butler contends. It is to expose the subjective conditions of neoliberal society without assuming that there is a "true" identity hidden below the deceptive logic of postracial enterprise culture. From this vantage point, we might ask somewhat different questions about ordinary people's performance on reality television.

To be sure, the industrial context of reality production constrains the ability to offer an account of oneself in the way Butler describes. As we have seen, "reality" is mediated and controlled at every stage, from casting to editing to marketing. However, culture is also messy and potentially unpredictable, and reality television is no exception. In my many years of watching reality television, I have certainly encountered small but powerful moments when ordinary people express the constraints within which they operate both as television performers and as social subjects. This might be the female contestant on a dating program who performs a saleable version of femininity in order to compete for the prize, but who also warily explains the rules of the game, and the role of women within it, and who gleefully steps outside her "role" when the bachelor is not around. Or it could be the impoverished black contestant on *From G's to Gents* who attempts to perform whiteness and class as demanded by lifestyle experts, but who shares an account of growing up poor and black that—even in its edited form—exposes the violence of this self-enterprising strategy. Unfortunately, glimpses of voice are fleeting and overshadowed by dominant lifestyle logics. Until the TV industry reflects on and questions its current investment in difference, this is not likely to change.

QUESTIONS FOR DISCUSSION

CHAPTER 1: BRANDING LIFESTYLE

1. How do brands of television differentiate themselves and encourage audiences to identify as brand communities? Watch a particular cable network for a period of time and visit its website to see how this is done.
2. Are there any lifestyle templates that cannot be successfully branded? What are television's priorities in establishing lifestyle brands?
3. What is the difference between a living brand and self-branding in the context of lifestyle and reality television? Discuss examples of both concepts and their potential overlap.

CHAPTER 2: THE SELF AS PROJECT

1. Pioneer Woman exemplifies how lifestyle television narrates and contributes to the disembedding and re-embedding of identity. What does this process involve, and what are some other salient examples?
2. Why is television interested in the ethics of self-fashioning and lifestyle? Does care of the self in mediated commercial culture work differently than in the ancient period studied by Foucault?
3. How do gender, race and class figure into the practices of self-making discussed in the chapter? What are the freedoms and limitations associated with the concept of the self as project?

CHAPTER 3: GOVERNING CITIZENS

1. Why is reality and lifestyle entertainment rarely associated with citizenship and democracy? Why is a reality entertainment program like *The Biggest Loser* more useful to neoliberal models of citizenship that value personal choice and responsibility than a documentary about food deserts?

2. Why has there recently been a surge in health-related lifestyle and reality television? Watch an episode of Dr. Oz or a program on the Discovery Health cable network and consider how it might operate as a technology of citizenship.

3. The governmental ambitions of MTV's teen pregnancy programs often contradict with the sexual behavior depicted on other reality programs and the celebrity afforded to the shows' young mothers. How might TV viewers navigate these mixed messages?

CHAPTER 4: THE LABOR OF LIFESTYLE

1. What are the different types of paid and unpaid labor associated with and enacted on lifestyle and reality television? Watch *America's Next Top Model* or another competition program and try to pinpoint the labor performed behind the scenes and on the show.

2. Compare and contrast an instructional cooking show geared to women with a reality show like *MasterChef* or *Hell's Kitchen*. To what extent are the programs gendered?

3. What do reality shows revolving around aesthetic and creative workers teach us about the conditions of work in postindustrial societies?

CHAPTER 5: PERFORMING DIFFERENCE

1. What are the "archetypes" in reality television programming today? What character types are casters looking for, and to what extent has this changed over the past five years?

2. Reality programs about the Amish have proliferated in recent years. How might the concept of Othering apply to these shows?

3. Are "accurate" representations of difference in reality television possible, or worth struggling over? Why, or why not?

BIBLIOGRAPHY

Acuna, Kirsten. 2012. "The 40-Year Transformation of How TLC Went From the Learning Channel to the Home of Honey Boo Boo." *Business Insider*, Nov. 28. http://www.businessinsider.com/history-of-tlc-from-learning-channel-to-honey-boo-boo-2012-11.

Adweek. 2012. "Bravo: Reaching the Affluencers." *Adweek*, April 23. http://www.adweek.com/sa-article/bravo-139587.

Affuso, Elizabeth. 2009. "Don't Just Watch It, Live It: Technology, Corporate Partnerships and The Hills." *Jump Cut: A Review of Contemporary Media* 51 (Spring). http://ejumpcut.org/archive/jc51.2009/Hills-Affuso/index.html.

Aitkenhead, Decca. 2010. "Hayley Taylor: 'I've felt what the unemployed feel: losing confidence, staring at four walls.'" *Guardian*, July 12. http://www.theguardian.com/tv-and-radio/2010/jul/12/hayley-taylor-fairy-jobmother-unemployment.

Allon, Fiona. 2010. "Speculating on Everyday Life: The Cultural Economy of the Quotidian." *Journal of Communication Inquiry* 34(4): 366–381.

Amaya, Hector. 2010. "Citizenship, Diversity, Law and Ugly Betty." *Media, Culture and Society* 32: 801–817.

Andrejevic, Mark. 2004. *Reality TV: The Work of Being Watched*. New York: Rowman & Littlefield.

Arcy, Jacquelyn. 2015. "Affective Enterprising: Branding the Self Through Emotional Excess." In *The Fantasy of Reality: Critical Essays on the Real Housewives*, ed. Rachel Silverman, 75–92. New York: Peter Lang.

Arvidsson, Adam. 2006. *Brands: Meaning and Value in Media Culture*. London: Routledge.

Banet-Weiser, Sarah. 2007a. *Kids Rule: Nickelodeon and Consumer Citizenship*. Durham, NC: Duke University Press.

Banet-Weiser, Sarah. 2007b. "What's Your Flava? Race and Postfeminism in Media Culture." In *Interrogating Postfeminism: Gender and the Politics of Popular Culture*, ed. Yvonne Tasker and Diane Negra, 202–226. Durham, NC: Duke University Press.

Banet-Weiser, Sarah. 2012. *Authentic TM: The Politics of Ambivalence in a Brand Culture*. New York: New York University Press.

Beck, Ulrich. 1994. "The Reinvention of Politics: Towards a Theory of Reflexive Modernization." In *Reflexive Modernization: Politics, Tradition and Aesthetics in the Modern Social Order*, ed. Ulrich Beck, Anthony Giddens and Scott Lash, 1–55. Stanford, CA: Stanford University Press.

Beck, Ulrich and Elisabeth Beck-Gernsheim. 2001. *Individualization: Institutionalized Individualism and Its Social and Political Consequences*. London: Sage.

Bell, David and Joanne Hollows. 2005. *Ordinary Lifestyles*. Maidenhead: Open University Press.

Bell, David and Joanne Hollows. 2009. *Historicizing Lifestyle: Mediating Taste, Consumption and Identity from the 1990s to the 1970s*. Aldershot: Ashgate.

Bennett, James. 2008. "The Television Personality System: Television Stardom Revisited After Film Theory." *Screen* 49(1): 32–50.

Bennett, Tony. 1998. *Culture: A Reformer's Science*. Thousand Oaks, CA: Sage.

Bentley, Fonzworth. 2007. *Advance Your Swagger: How to Use Manners, Confidence, and Style to Get Ahead*. New York: Villard.

Berger, John. 1972/1990. *Ways of Seeing*. New York: Penguin.

Berlant, Lauren. 2011. *Cruel Optimism*. Durham, NC: Duke University Press.

Bettie, Julie. 2000. "Women Without Class: Chicas, Cholas, Trash, and the Presence/Absence of Class Identity." *Signs* 26(1): 1–35.

Bignell, Jonathan. 2014. "Realism and Reality Formats." In *A Companion to Reality Television*, ed. Laurie Ouellette, 97–115. Malden, MA: Wiley.

Binkley, Sam. 2007a. "Governmentality and Lifestyle Studies." *Sociology Compass* 1(1): 11–126.

Binkley, Sam. 2007b. *Getting Loose: Lifestyle Consumption in the 1970s*. Durham, NC: Duke University Press.

Boltanski, Luc and Eve Chiapello. 2007. *The New Spirit of Capitalism*. London: Verso.

Bonner, Frances. 2003. *Ordinary Television: Analyzing Popular TV*. London: Sage.

Bourdieu, Pierre. 1984. *Distinction: A Social Critique of the Judgment of Taste*. Cambridge: Cambridge University Press.

Bragg, Sara. 2006. "Young Women, the Media and Sex Education." *Feminist Media Studies* 6(4): 546–551.

Brunsdon, Charlotte. 2003. "Lifestyling Britain: The 8–9 Slot on British Television." *International Journal of Cultural Studies* 6(1): 5–23.

Brunsdon, Charlotte. 2004. "Taste and Time on Television." *Screen* 45(2): 115–129.

Burchell, Graham. 1996. "Liberal Government and Techniques of the Self." In *Foucault and Political Reason: Liberalism, Neo-Liberalism and Rationalities of Government*, ed. Andrew Barry, Thomas Osbourne and Nikolas Rose, 19–36. Chicago, IL: University of Chicago Press.

Butler, Judith. 1990. *Gender Trouble: Gender and the Subversion of Identity*. New York: Routledge.

Butler, Judith. 2005. *Giving an Account of Oneself*. New York: Fordham University Press.

Byars, Jackie and Eileen Meehan. 1944–95. "Once in a Lifetime: Constructing the Working Woman through Cable Narrowcasting." *Camera Obscura* 33–34: 213–241.

Campbell, Colin. 1987. *The Romantic Ethic and the Spirit of Modern Consumerism*. Oxford: Basil Blackwell.

Carter, Bill. 2013. "A Calculated Push into Entertainment Lifts Duck Dynasty Family's Fortunes." *New York Times*, Aug. 25. https://www.google.com/?gws_rd=ssl#q=New+York+Times%2C+Bill+Carter%2C+A+Calculated+Push+Into+Entertainment+Lifts+Duck+Dynasty+Family%E2%80%99s+Fortunes.

Cassidy, Marsha. 2005. *What Women Watched: Daytime Television in the 1950s*. Austin, TX: University of Texas Press.

Chaney, David. 1996. *Lifestyles*. London: Routledge.

Chaney, David. 2000. "From Ways of Life to Lifestyle: Rethinking Culture as Ideology and Sensibility." In *Culture in the Communication Age*, ed. James Lull, 75–88. London: Routledge.

Cohen, Lizbeth. 2003. *A Consumer's Republic: The Politics of Mass Consumption in Postwar America*. New York: Vintage.

Collins, Kathleen. 2009. *Watching What We Eat: The Evolution of Television Cooking Shows*. New York: Continuum.

Congressional Research Service. 2011. "Teenage Pregnancy Prevention Statistics and Programs." Feb. 3. http://www.loc.gov/crsinfo/.

Copple-Smith, Erin. 2012. "'Affluencers' by Bravo: Defining an Audience Through Cross-Promotion." *Popular Communication* 10(4): 286–301.

Corner, John. 2002. "Performing the Real: Documentary Diversions." *Television & New Media* 3(3): 255–269.

Couldry, Nick. 2010. *Why Voice Matters: Culture and Politics After Neoliberalism*. London: Sage.

Cox, Nicole and Jennifer M. Proffitt. 2012. "The Housewives' Guide to Better Living: Promoting Consumption on Bravo's *The Real Housewives*." *Communication, Culture & Critique* 5(2): 295–312.

Curtin, Michael and Jane Shattuc. 2009. *The American Television Industry*. London: British Film Institute.

Daems, Jim. 2014. *The Makeup of RuPaul's Drag Race: Essays on the Queen of Reality Shows*. Jefferson, NC: McFarland.

Davila, Arlene. 2001. *Latinos, Inc.: The Making and Marketing of a People*. Berkeley, CA: University of California Press.

de Solier, Isabelle. 2005. "TV Dinners: Culinary Television, Education and Distinction." *Continuum: Journal of Media & Cultural Studies* 19(4): 465–481.

Deery, June. 2012. *Consuming Reality: The Commercialization of Factual Entertainment*. New York: Palgrave Macmillan.

Deery, June. 2015. *Reality TV*. Cambridge: Polity.

Diamond, Elin. 1996. "Introduction: Performance and Cultural Politics." In *Performance and Cultural Politics*, ed. Elin Diamond, 1–12. New York and London: Routledge.

Dominus, Susan. 2008. "The Affluencer." *New York Times*, Oct. 30. http://www.nytimes.com/2008/11/02/magazine/02zalaznick-t.html?pagewanted=all&_r=0.

Dovey, Jon. 2000. *Freakshow: First Person Media and Factual Television*. London: Pluto Press.

Duggan, Lisa. 2004. *The Twilight of Inequality: Neoliberalism, Cultural Politics and the Attack on Democracy*. Boston, MA: Beacon Press.

Featherstone, Mike. 1991. *Consumer Culture and Postmodernism*. London: Sage.

Florida, Richard. 2002. *The Rise of the Creative Class*. New York: Basic Books.

Foucault, Michel. 1980. "Two Lectures." In *Power/Knowledge*, ed. Colin Gordon, 78–108. New York: Pantheon.

Foucault, Michel. 1984. "On the Genealogy of Ethics." In *The Foucault Reader*, ed. Paul Rabinow, 350–373. New York: Penguin.

Foucault, Michel. 1985. *The History of Sexuality, Vol. 2: The Care of the Self*. New York: Vintage.

Foucault, Michel. 1986. *The History of Sexuality, Vol. 3: The Use of Pleasure*. New York: Vintage.

Foucault, Michel. 1988. "Technologies of the Self." In *Technologies of the Self: A Seminar with Michel Foucault*, ed. Luther Martin, Huck Gutman and Patrick Hutton, 16–49. Amherst, MA: University of Massachusetts Press.

Foucault, Michel. 1991. "Governmentality." In *The Foucault Effect: Studies in Governmentality*, ed. Graham Burchell, Colin Gordon and Peter Miller, 87–104. Chicago, IL: University of Chicago Press.

Foucault, Michel. 1997. "The Ethics of the Concern of the Self as a Practice of Freedom." In *Ethics*, ed. Paul Rabinow, 281–301. New York: Free Press.

Foucault, Michel. 2010. *The Birth of Biopolitics: Lectures at the College de France, 1978–1979*. New York: Palgrave Macmillan.

Fraser, Nancy and Linda Gordon. 1977. "A Genealogy of Dependency: Tracing a Keyword of the U.S. Welfare State." In *Nancy Fraser, Justice Interruptus: Critical Reflections on the Postsocialist Condition*, 121–150. New York: Routledge.

Gamson, Joshua. 1999. *Freaks Talk Back: Talk Shows and Sexual Nonconformity*. Chicago, IL: University of Chicago Press.

Gamson, Joshua. 2014. "'It's Been a While Since I've Seen, Like, Straight People': Queer Visibility in the Age of Postnetwork Reality Television." In *A Companion to Reality Television*, ed. Laurie Ouellette, 227–246. Malden, MA, and Oxford: Wiley.

Gauntlett, David. 2008. *Media, Gender and Identity: An Introduction*. London: Routledge.

Giddens, Anthony. 1991. *Modernity and Self-Identity: Self and Society in the Late Modern Age*. Stanford, CA: Stanford University Press.

Gil, Tiffany Melissa. 2001. "'I Had My Own Business . . . So I Didn't Have to Worry': Beauty Salons, Beauty Culturalists and the Politics of African American Female Entrepreneurship." In *Beauty and Business: Commerce, Gender and Culture in Modern America*, ed. Philip Scranton, 169–194. New York: Routledge.

Gil, Tiffany Melissa. 2010. *Beauty Shop Politics: African American Women's Activism in the Beauty Industry*. Urbana, IL: University of Illinois Press.

Gill, Rosalind. 2007. "Postfeminist Media Culture: Elements of a Sensibility." *European Journal of Cultural Studies* 10(2): 147–166.

Gill, Rosalind and Andy Pratt. 2008. "In the Social Factory? Immaterial Labor, Precariousness and Cultural Work." *Theory, Culture & Society* 25(1): 1–30.

Gill, Rosalind, Christina Scharff and Ana Sophia Elias, eds. 2016. *Aesthetic Labour: Rethinking Beauty Politics in Neoliberalism*. London: Palgrave Macmillan.

Gordon, Colin. 1991. "Governmental Rationality: An Introduction." In *The Foucault Effect*, ed. Graham Burchell, Colin Gordon and Peter Miller, 1–54. Chicago, IL: University of Chicago Press.

Gray, Herman. 2013. "Subject(ed) to Recognition." *American Quarterly* 65(4): 771–798.

Griffiths, Allison. 2001. *Wondrous Difference: Cinema, Anthropology and Turn of the Century Visual Culture*. New York: Columbia University Press.

Grindstaff, Laura. 2002. *The Money Shot: Class, Trash and the Making of Daytime Talk Shows.* Chicago, IL: University of Chicago Press.

Grindstaff, Laura. 2009. "Self-Serve Celebrity: The Production of Ordinariness and the Ordinariness of Production in Reality Television." In *Production Studies: Cultural Studies of Media Industries*, ed. Vicki Mayer, Miranda J. Banks and John T. Caldwell, 71–86. New York: Routledge.

Grindstaff, Laura. 2011a. "From Jerry Springer to Jersey Shore: The Cultural Politics of Class In/On U.S. Reality Programming." In *Reality Television and Class*, ed. Beverly Skeggs and Helen Wood, 197–209. London: Palgrave Macmillan.

Grindstaff, Laura. 2011b. "Just Be Yourself—Only More So: Ordinary Celebrity in the Era of Self-Service Television." In *The Politics of Reality Television: Global Perspectives*, ed. Marwan Kraidy and Katherine Sender, 44–57. London and New York: Routledge.

Grindstaff, Laura. 2014. "DI(t)Y, Reality Style: The Cultural Work of Ordinary Celebrity." In *A Companion to Reality Television*, ed. Laurie Ouellette, 324–344. Malden, MA, and Oxford: Wiley.

Grindstaff, Laura and Susan Murray. 2015. "Reality Celebrity: Branded Affect and the Emotion Economy." *Public Culture* 27(1): 109–135.

Hamad, Hannah. 2014. "Fairy Jobmother to the Rescue: Postfeminism and the Recessionary Cultures of Reality TV." In *Gendering the Recession: Media and Culture in the Age of Austerity*, ed. Diane Negra and Yvonne Tasker, 223–245. Durham, NC: Duke University Press.

Hampp, Andrew. 2011. "Bravo's Buzz Marketing Keeps Viewers Tuned In." *Ad Age*, April 11. http://adage.com/article/cmo-interviews/bravo-s-buzz-marketing-viewers-tuned/226898/.

Hardt, Michael. 1999. "Affective Labor." *boundary 2* 26(2): 89–100.

Harvey, David. 2004. "The 'New' Imperialism: Accumulation by Dispossession." *Socialist Register* 40: 63–87.

Harvey, David. 2005. *A Brief History of Neoliberalism.* Oxford: Oxford University Press.

Hasinoff, Amy. 2008. "Fashioning Race for the Free Market on America's Next Top Model." *Critical Studies in Media Communication* 25(3): 324–343.

Hawkins, Gay. 2001. "The Ethics of Television." *International Journal of Cultural Studies* 4(4): 412–436.

Hay, James. 2010. "Too Good to Fail: Managing Financial Crisis Through the Moral Economy of Reality TV." *Journal of Communication Inquiry* 34(4): 382–402.

Hearn, Alison. 2006. "John, a 20-year-old Boston Native with a 'Great Sense of Humour': On the Spectacularization of the 'Self' and the Incorporation of Identity in the Age of Reality Television." *International Journal of Media and Cultural Politics* 2(2): 131–147.

Hearn, Alison. 2008. "Meat, Mask, Burden: Probing the Contours of the Branded Self." *Journal of Consumer Culture* 8(2): 197–217.

Hearn, Alison. 2010. "Reality Television, The Hills and the Limits of the Immaterial Labor Thesis." *tripleC* 8(1): 60–76.

Heller, Dana, ed. 2006. *The Great American Makeover: Television, History, Nation*. New York: Palgrave Macmillan.

Hill, Annette. 2007. *Restyling Factual TV: Audiences and News, Documentary and Reality Genres*. London: Routledge.

Hochschild, Arlie. 1983/2003. *The Managed Heart: Commercialization of Human Feeling*. Berkeley, CA: University of California Press.

Hochschild, Arlie. 1989/2003. *The Second Shift*. Penguin: New York.

Hollows, Joanne. 2003. "Oliver's Twist: Leisure, Labor and Domestic Masculinity in the Naked Chef." *International Journal of Cultural Studies* 6(2): 229–248.

Hollows, Joanne. 2008. *Domestic Cultures*. Maidenhead: Open University Press.

hooks, bell. 1992. *Black Looks: Race and Representation*. Boston, MA: South End Press.

Jenkins, Henry. 2006. *Convergence Culture*. New York: NYU Press.

Jenkins, Henry. 2013. "Thinking Critically About Brand Cultures: An Interview with Sarah Banet-Weiser." *Confessions of an Aca-Fan*, April 10. http://henryjenkins.org/2013/04/thinking-critically-about-brand-cultures-an-interview-with-sarah-banet-weiser-part-one.html.

Johnson, Blanche. 2015. "Do TLC's Makeover Shows Do More Harm Than Good?" *Fox News*, June 15. http://www.foxnews.com/entertainment/2015/06/15/do-tlc-makeover-shows-do-more-harm-than-good/.

Johnson, Catherine. 2012. *Branding Television*. London: Routledge.

Johnson, Victoria E. 2013. "Monday Night Football: Brand Identity." In *How to Watch Television*, ed. Ethan Thompson and Jason Mittell, 253–270. New York: NYU Press.

Joseph, Ralina. 2012. *Transcending Blackness: From the New Millennium Mulatta to the Exceptional Multiracial*. Durham, NC: Duke University Press.

Keane, Michael and Albert Moran. 2008. "Television's New Engines." *Television and New Media* 9(2): 155–169.

Krasewski, Jon. 2009. "Country Hicks and Urban Cliques: Mediating Race, Reality and Liberalism on MTV's The Real World." In *Reality TV: Remaking Television Culture* (2nd edition), ed. Susan Murray and Laurie Ouellette, 205–222. New York: New York University Press.

Lazzarato, Maurizio. 2006. "Immaterial Labour." In *Radical Thought in Italy: A Potential Politics*, ed. Paul Virno and Michael Hardt, 133–150. Minneapolis, MN: University of Minnesota Press.

Lears, Jackson T.J. 1983. "From Salvation to Self-Realization: Advertising and the Therapeutic Roots of the Consumer Culture, 1880–1930." In *The Culture of Consumption*, ed. Richard Wightman Fox and T.J. Jackson Lears, 3–38. New York: Pantheon.

Lemke, Thomas. 2011. *Biopolitics: An Advanced Introduction*. New York: NYU Press.

Lewis, Tania. 2008. *Smart Living: Lifestyle Media and Popular Expertise*. New York: Peter Lang.

Lewis, Tania. 2010. "Branding, Celebritization and the Lifestyle Expert." *Cultural Studies* 24(4): 580–598.

Lotz, Amanda. 2006. *Redesigning Women: Television After the Network Era*. Urbana, IL: University of Illinois Press.

Lowry, Brian. 2013. "TV Review: 'Welcome to Myrtle Manor'." *Variety*, Feb. 27. http://variety.com/2013/tv/reviews/tv-review-welcome-to-myrtle-manor-820780/.

Lury, Celia. 2004. *Brands: The Logos of the Global Economy*. London: Routledge.

Lury, Celia. 2011. *Consumer Culture* (2nd edition). New Brunswick, NJ: Rutgers University Press.

Madison, Soyini D. and Judith Hamera. 2005. "Introduction: Performance at the Intersections." In *The Sage Handbook of Performance Studies*, ed. D. Soyini Madison and Judith Hamera, xi–xxv. Thousand Oaks, CA: Sage.

Maguire, Jennifer Smith. 2008. *Fit for Consumption: Sociology and the Business of Fitness*. New York: Routledge.

Mandziuk, Roseann M. 2001. "Confessional Discourse and Modern Desires: Power and Please in True Story Magazine." *Critical Studies in Media Communication* 18(2): 174–193.

Maslin Nir, Sarah. 2015. "The Price of Nice Nails." *New York Times*, May 7. http://www.nytimes.com/2015/05/10/nyregion/at-nail-salons-in-nyc-manicurists-are-underpaid-and-unprotected.html?_r=0.

Mayer, Vicki. 2011. "Reality Television's Class Rooms: Knowing, Showing and Telling about Social Class in Reality Casting Labor and the College Classroom." In *Reality Television and Class*, ed. Helen Wood and Beverly Skeggs, 185–196. London: Palgrave Macmillan.

Mayer, Vicki. 2014. "Cast-aways: The Plights and Pleasures of Reality Casting and Production Studies." In *A Companion to Reality Television*, ed. Laurie Ouellette, 57–73. Malden, MA, and Oxford: Wiley.

McElroy, Ruth. 2008. "Property TV: The (Re)Making of Home on National Screens." *European Journal of Cultural Studies* 11(1): 43–61.

McGee, Micki. 2005. *Self-help, Inc: Makeover Culture in American Life.* New York: Oxford University Press.

McGraw, Phillip. 1999. *Life Strategies: Doing What Works, Doing What Matters.* New York: Hyperion Books.

McRobbie, Angela. 2002. "From Holloway to Hollywood: Happiness at Work in the New Cultural Economy." In *Cultural Economy: Cultural Analysis and Commercial Life*, ed. Paul du Gay and Michael Pryke, 97–114. London: Sage.

McRobbie, Angela. 2007. "Top Girls: Young Women and the New Sexual Contract." *Cultural Studies* 21(4–5): 718–737.

McRobbie, Angela. 2010. *The Aftermath of Feminism: Gender, Culture and Social Change.* London: Sage.

McRuer, Robert. 2006. *Crip Theory: Cultural Signs of Queerness and Disability.* New York: NYU Press.

Mears, Ashley. 2014. "Aesthetic Labor for the Sociologies of Work, Gender and Beauty." *Sociology Compass* 8(12): 1330–1343.

Meyer, Madonna Harrington. 2000. "Introduction." In *Care Work: Gender, Class and the Welfare State*, ed. Madonna Harington Mayer, 1–6. New York: Routledge.

Miller, Toby. 2007. *Cultural Citizenship: Cosmopolitanism, Consumerism and Television in a Neoliberal Age.* Philadelphia, PA: Temple University Press.

Moran, Albert. 2012. *Understanding the Global TV Format.* Bristol: Intellect Ltd.

Moran, Albert. 2014. "Program Format Franchising in the Age of Reality Television." In *A Companion to Reality Television*, ed. Laurie Ouellette, 74–94. Malden, MA, and Oxford: Wiley.

Mosley, Rachel. 2000. "Makeover Takeover on British Television." *Screen* 41(3): 299–314.

Mueller, Gavin. 2012. "Reality TV and the Flexible Future." *Jacobin* 6 (Spring). https://www.jacobinmag.com/2012/10/reality-t-v-and-flexible-future/.

Mukherjee, Roopali. 2011. "Bling-Fling: Commodity Consumption and the Politics of the 'Post-Racial'." In *Critical Rhetorics of Race*, ed. Michael Lacey and Kent Ono, 178–196. New York: NYU Press.

Mulvey, Laura. 1993. "Some Thoughts on Theories of Fetishism in the Context of Contemporary Culture." *October* 65 (Summer): 3–20.

Nadesan, Majia Holmer. 2008. *Governmentality, Biopower and Everyday Life.* New York: Routledge.

Nadesan, Maja Holmer. 2010. *Governing Childhood into the 21st Century.* New York: Palgrave Macmillan.

Nathanson, Elizabeth. 2013. *Television and Postfeminist Housekeeping: No Time for Mother*. New York: Routledge.

National Campaign to Prevent Teen and Unplanned Pregnancy. 2009. "Socio-Economic and Family Characteristics of Teen Childbearing," Sept. http://www.thenationalcampaign.org/.

Neff, Gina. 2012. *Venture Labor: Work and the Burden of Risk in Innovative Industries*. Cambridge, MA: MIT Press.

Neff, Gina, Elizabeth Wissinger and Sharon Zukin. 2005. "Entrepreneurial Labor among Cultural Producers: 'Cool' Jobs in 'Hot' Industries." *Social Semiotics* 15(3): 307–334.

Negra, Diane. 2013. "Gender Bifurcation in the Recessionary Economy: Extreme Couponing and Gold Rush Alaska." *Cinema Journal* 53(1): 123–129.

Negra, Diane and Yvonne Tasker, ed. 2014. *Gendering the Recession: Media and Culture in the Age of Austerity*. Durham, NC: Duke University Press.

Nettleton, Sarah. 1997. "Governing the Risky Self: How to Become Healthy, Wealthy and Wise." In *Foucault, Health and Medicine*, ed. Alan Peterson and Robin Bunton, 189–206. London: Routledge.

Newman, Michael Z. 2013. "Everyday Italian: Cultivating Taste." In *How to Watch Television*, ed. Ethan Thompson and Jason Mittell, 330–337. New York: NYU Press.

Newman, Michael Z. and Elana Levine. 2011. *Legitimating Television: Media Convergence and Cultural Status*. New York: Routledge.

Nichols, Bill. 1994. *Blurred Boundaries: Questions of Meaning in Contemporary Culture*. Bloomington, IN: Indiana University Press.

Nicoară, Mona. 2012. "American Gypsies Needs to Catch Up With the Reality of Roma People's Lives." *Guardian*, July 28. www.theguardian.com/commentisfree/2012/jul/28/american-gypsies-reality-roma-lives.

O'Reagan, Tom, Mark Balnaves and Jason Sternberg. 2002. *Mobilising the Audience*. Brisbane: University of Queensland Press.

Ouellette, Laurie. 2002. *Viewers Like You? How Public TV Failed the People*. New York: Columbia University Press.

Ouellette, Laurie. 2009. "Reinventing PBS: Public Television in a Post-Network, Post-Welfare Era." In *Beyond Primetime: Television Programming in the Post-Network Era*, ed. Amanda Lotz, 180–202. New York: Routledge.

Ouellette, Laurie. 2011. "Real Justice: Law and Order on Reality Television." In *Imagining Legality: Where Law Meets Popular Culture*, ed. Austin Sarat, 152–176. Tuscaloosa, AL: University of Alabama Press.

Ouellette, Laurie. 2014a. "Enterprising Selves: Reality Television and Human Capital." In *Making Media Work: Cultures of Management in the Entertainment Industries*, ed. Derek Johnson, Derek Kompare and Avi Santo, 90–112. New York: NYU Press.

Ouellette, Laurie. 2014b. "It's Not TV, It's Birth Control: Reality Television and the 'Problem' of Teenage Pregnancy." In *Reality Gendervision: Gender and Sexuality on Transatlantic Reality Television*, ed. Brenda Weber, 236–258. Durham, NC: Duke University Press.

Ouellette, Laurie. 2016 (forthcoming). "Dream Jobs: The Glamorization of Beauty Service Labor in Media Culture." In *Aesthetic Labour: Rethinking Beauty Politics in Neoliberalism*, ed. Rosalind Gill, Christina Scharff and Ana Sophia Elias. London: Palgrave Macmillan.

Ouellette, Laurie and Jacquelyn Arcy. 2015. "Live Through This: Feminist Care of the Self 2.0." *Frame: Journal of Literary Studies* 28(1): 95–114.

Ouellette, Laurie and James Hay. 2008. *Better Living Through Reality TV: Television and Post-Welfare Citizenship*. Malden, MA: Blackwell.

Ouellette, Laurie and Julie Wilson. 2011. "Women's Work: Affective Labor and Convergence Culture." *Cultural Studies* 25(4–5): 548–565.

Page, Allison. 2015. "Advance Your Freedom: Race, Enterprise and Neoliberal Governmentality on From G's to Gents." *Television and New Media* 16(5): 439–453.

Palmer, Gareth. 2004. "'The New You': Class and Transformation in Lifestyle Television." In *Understanding Reality Television*, ed. Su Holmes and Debora Jermyn, 173–190. London: Routledge.

Palmer, Gareth, ed. 2008. *Exposing Lifestyle Television: The Big Reveal*. Farnham: Ashgate.

Pramaggiore, Maria and Diane Negra. 2014. "Keeping Up With the Aspirations: Commercial Family Values and the Kardashian Brand." In *Reality Gendervision: Gender and Sexuality on Transatlantic Reality Television*, ed. Brenda Weber, 76–96. Durham, NC: Duke University Press.

Patten, Dominic and David Robb. 2015. "'Marriage Boot Camp' Strike Over." *Deadline*, June 23. http://deadline.com/2015/06/marriage-boot-camp-strike-editors-thinkfactory-media-1201452431/.

Perlman, Allison. 2012. "Whitewashing Diversity: The Conservative Attack on the 'Stealth Fairness Doctrine'." *Television and New Media* 13(4): 353–373.

Pew Research Social and Demographic Trends. 2012. "The New Demography of American Motherhood." http://www.pewsocialtrends.org/2010/05/06/the-new-demography-of-american-motherhood/.

Polan, Dana. 2011. *Julia Child's The French Chef*. Durham, NC: Duke University Press.

Postrel, Virginia. 2004. *The Substance of Style: How the Rise of Aesthetic Consciousness is Remaking Commerce, Culture and Consciousness*. New York: Harper Perennial.

Raphael, Chad. 2009. "The Political Economic Origins of Reali-TV." In *Reality TV: Remaking Television Culture* (2nd edition), eds. Susan Murray and Laurie Ouellette, 123–141. New York: NYU Press.

Read, Jason. 2009. "A Genealogy of Homo-Economicus: Neoliberalism and the Production of Subjectivity." *Foucault Studies* 6: 25–36.

Rose, Nikolas. 1992. "Governing the Enterprising Self." In *The Values of the Enterprise Culture*, ed. Paul Heelas and Paul Morris, 141–164. London: Routledge.

Rose, Nikolas. 1996. "Governing 'Advanced' Liberal Democracies." In *Foucault and Political Reason: Liberalism, Neo-Liberalism and Rationalities of Government*, ed. Andrew Barry, Thomas Osbourne and Nikolas Rose, 37–64. Chicago, IL: University of Chicago Press.

Rose, Nikolas. 1998. *Inventing Ourselves: Psychology, Power and Personhood*. Cambridge: Cambridge University Press.

Rose, Nikolas. 1999. *Powers of Freedom: Reframing Political Thought*. Cambridge: Cambridge University Press.

Ross, Andrew. 2010. *Nice Work If You Can Get It: Life and Labor in Precarious Times*. New York: NYU Press.

Ruby, Jay. "Speaking For, Speaking About, Speaking With, or Speaking Alongside: An Anthropological and Documentary Dilemma." *Journal of Film and Video Studies* 44(1–2): 42–66.

Ruoff, Jeff. 2001. *American Family: A Televised Life*. Minneapolis, MN: University of Minnesota Press.

RuPaul. 2010. *Workin' It: RuPaul's Guide to Life, Liberty and the Pursuit of Style*. New York: It Books.

Ryan, Maureen. 2015a. "Entertaining Fantasies: Lifestyle and Social Life in 1980s America." *Journal of Communication Inquiry* 39(1): 82–101.

Ryan, Maureen. 2015b. "Logics of Lifestyle and the Rise of the Scripps Networks, 1994–2010." *Feminist Media Histories* 1(2): 37–63.

Said, Edward. 1979. *Orientalism*. New York: Vintage.

Schwartz, John. 2014. "Polygamy as Lifestyle Choice, and a Reality TV Brand." *New York Times*, Jan. 8. http://www.nytimes.com/2014/01/09/us/polygamy-as-a-lifestyle-choice-and-a-reality-tv-brand-name.html?_r=0.

Sender, Katherine. 2005. "Queens for a Day: Queer Eye for the Straight Guy and the Neoliberal Project." *Critical Studies in Media Communication* 23(2): 131–151.

Sender, Katherine. 2012. *The Makeover: Reality Television and Reflexive Audiences*. New York: NYU Press.

Shattuc, Jane. 1997. *The Talking Cure: TV Talk Shows and Women*. New York: Routledge.

Skeggs, Beverly and Helen Wood. 2011. "Introduction: Real Class." In *Reality Television and Class*, ed. Helen Wood and Beverly Skeggs, 1–32. London: Palgrave Macmillan.

Skeggs, Beverly and Helen Wood. 2012. *Reacting to Reality Television: Performance, Audience and Value*. London: Routledge.

Smith-Shomade, Baretta. 2007. *Pimpin Ain't Easy: Selling Black Entertainment Television*. New York: Routledge.

Solinger, Ricki. 1992/2000. *Wake Up Little Susie: Single Pregnancy and Race Before Roe v. Wade*. New York: Routledge.

Spigel, Lynn. 1992. *Make Room for TV: Television and the Family Ideal in Postwar America*. Chicago, IL: University of Chicago Press.

Squires, Catherine. 2014. "The Conundrum of Race and Reality Television." In *A Companion to Reality Television*, ed. Laurie Ouellette, 247–263. Malden, MA, and Oxford: Wiley.

Swenson, Rebecca. 2009. "Domestic Divo? Televised Treatments of Masculinity, Femininity and Food." *Critical Studies in Media Communication* 26(1): 36–53.

Szuchman, Paula and Jenny Anderson. 2011. *Spousonomics: Using Economics to Master Love, Marriage and Dirty Dishes*. New York: Random House.

Taylor, Lisa. 2002. "From Ways of Life to Lifestyle: The 'Ordinari-ization' of British Gardening Television." *European Journal of Communication* 14(4): 479–495.

Terranova, Tiziana. 2000. "Free Labor: Producing Culture for the Digital Economy." *Social Text* 18(2): 33–58.

Turner, Graeme. 2006. "The Mass Production of Celebrity: 'Celetoids', Reality TV and the 'Demotic Turn'." *International Journal of Cultural Studies* 9(2): 153–165.

Turner, Graeme. 2010. *Ordinary People and the Media: The Demotic Turn*. Thousand Oaks, CA: Sage.

Turner, Graeme. 2014. "Reality Television and the Demotic Turn." In *A Companion to Reality Television*, ed. Laurie Ouellette, 309–323. Malden, MA, and Oxford: Wiley.

Turow, Joseph. 1997. *Breaking Up America: Advertisers and the New Media World*. Chicago, IL: University of Chicago Press.

Walkerdine, Valerie. 2003. "Reclassifying Upward Mobility: Femininity and the Neo-Liberal Subject." *Gender and Education* 15(3): 237–248.

Ward, Kate. 2011. "Bravo Boasts the Most Effective Product Placement." *Entertainment Weekly*, April 29. http://www.ew.com/article/2011/04/29/bravo-product-placement.

Watts, Amber. 2006. "Remaking Consumer Culture, One Woman at a Time." In *The Great American Makeover: Television, History, Nation*, ed. Dana Heller, 141–158. New York: Palgrave Macmillan.

Weber, Brenda. 2009. *Makeover TV: Selfhood, Citizenship and Celebrity*. Durham, NC: Duke University Press.

Weber, Max. 1992. *The Protestant Ethic and the Spirit of Capitalism*. New York: Routledge.

White, Mimi. 1992. *Tele-Advising: Therapeutic Discourse in American Television*. Chapel Hill, NC: University of North Carolina Press.

White, Mimi. 2014. "House Hunters, Real Estate Television and Everyday Cosmopolitanism." In *A Companion to Reality Television*, ed. Laurie Ouellette, 386–401. Malden, MA, and Oxford: Wiley.

Willett, Julie A. (2000). *Permanent Waves: The Making of the American Beauty Shop*. New York: NYU Press.

Williams, Raymond. 1992. *Television: Technology and Cultural Form*. Hanover, NH: Wesleyan University Press.

Wood, Helen and Beverly Skeggs. 2004. "Notes on Ethical Scenarios of Self on British Reality TV." *Feminist Media Studies* 4(2): 205–208.

Zimmerman, Heidi. 2015. "Branding Environmentalism for TV: The Rise and Fall of Planet Green." Ph.D. Dissertation, University of Minnesota. August.

VIDEOGRAPHY

The following videography provides information about the production companies, distributors and TV networks associated with the programs discussed in this book. I have also provided a brief synopsis of the shows.

While this list presents a starting point for viewing and research, it is by no means exhaustive. By the time this book appears in print, new lifestyle-themed programs will inevitably have appeared; some will have been cancelled (but perhaps still shown in re-runs) and emerging clusters of significance will require further critical analysis.

Because *Lifestyle TV* focuses on the lifestyling of television in the U.S., most of the productions cited below are U.S.-based (some with international distribution), and do not represent the phenomenon of lifestyle television worldwide. Some of the U.S. programs discussed in this book are based on global formats adapted in slightly different ways across a wide range of local contexts. I have noted these cases—as well as the national origins of programs that do not originate in the United States.

16 and Pregnant (2009-present). 11th Street Productions/MTV Remote Productions/ MTV. Real stories about teenage pregnancy.

30 Minute Meals (2001-present). Food Network. Time-saving cooking instruction with host Rachel Ray.

All-American Muslim (2011). Shed Media/Discovery Communications/TLC. Reality series about Lebanese-American Muslim family, controversially cancelled after one season.

An American Family (1973). WNET/PBS. Serialized documentary following the daily lives of a Southern California family. Considered an early precursor of reality TV.

American Gypsies (2012). Stick Figure Productions/National Geographic. Reality series about New York family with Roma heritage.

American Trucker (2011). Brentwood Communications International/Speed Channel. True stories about truck drivers.

America's Next Top Model (2003–15). 10 by 10 Entertainment/Pottle Productions/Ty Ty Baby Productions/UPN/CW. Competition for aspiring fashion models.

Amish Mafia (2012–15). Hot Snakes Media/Discovery Channel. Reality series about purported thugs in Amish community.

The Baby Borrowers (2008). Love Productions/NBC. Social experiment designed to deter teenage pregnancy.

Barefoot Contessa (2002-present). Food Network. Instruction on cooking and entertaining with host Ina Garten.

Basketball Wives (2010–13). Shed Media/VH1. Reality series about the female partners of U.S. basketball stars.

Benefit Busters (2009). Studio Lambert/Channel 4. U.K. reality series about people expected to transition off government assistance.

Benefits Street (2014–15). Love Productions/Channel 4. U.K. documentary series about welfare recipients.

Bethenny Ever After (2010–12). Shed Media/Bravo. Spin-off of *Real Housewives of New York* following cast member Bethenny Frankel.

Bethenny Getting Married (2010). Shed Media/Bravo. Spin-off of *Real Housewives of New York* following cast member Bethenny Frankel.

Big Brother (2000-present). Endemol/Shapiro/Grodner Productions/Evolution Film & Tape/CBS. Social experiment/reality game show. Based on global format.

Big Fat Gypsy Weddings (2010–12). Firecracker Films/Channel 4. U.K. reality series about wedding preparations in Roma and Traveller communities.

Big Sexy (2011). Atlas Media/TLC. Reality series about plus-sized women working in the fashion industry.

The Biggest Loser (2004-present). 25/7 Productions/NBC Universal Television Distribution/NBC. Weight loss competition. Based on global format.

Blow Out (2004–06). Magna Global Entertainment/Reveille Productions/Shapiro/Grodner Productions/Bravo. Reality series set in Beverly Hills hair salon.

B.O.R.N. to Style (2014-present). Left/Right Features/FYI. Reality series about fashion stylists in Harlem.

Breaking Amish (2012-present). Hot Snakes Media/Discovery Communications/TLC. Reality series about Amish and Mennonite young people who move to New York City.

Breaking Amish: LA (2013). Hot Snakes Media/Discovery Communications/TLC. Spin-off of *Breaking Amish*.

Bridalplasty (2010). 51 Minds Entertainment/E! Entertainment Television. Competition/ makeover program for brides.

Brides Gone Styled (2015-present). Half Yard Productions/Discovery Communications/TLC. Makeover program for brides.

Charm School (2007–09). 51 Minds Entertainment/VH1. Competition/makeover program. Spin-off of dating competition *Flavor of Love*.

The Chew (2011-present). Chew Production/ABC. Daytime instruction and commentary on food, cooking and entertainment.

Chopped (2007-present). City Lights Media/Food Network. Cooking competition for professional chefs.

Clean House (2003–11) E! Entertainment Television/Style Network. Home makeover focused on combatting clutter.

Coal (2011). Original Productions/Spike TV. Reality series about coal miners.

Color Splash (2007). Edelman Productions/Johlt Productions/HGTV. Home makeover.

Cupcake Wars (2009–13). Super Delicious Productions/Food Network. Competition for professional bakers.

Curb Appeal (1999–2011). Edelman Productions/HGTV. Home makeover.

Cutting It in the ATL (2015-present). Leftfield Pictures/Women's Entertainment Television (WE). Reality series about competitive hairstylists in Atlanta.

Dad Camp (2010). 3 Ball Productions/VH1. Social experiment targeting young unmarried dads.

Dance Moms (2011-present). Collins Avenue Productions/Lifetime. Reality show about child dancers and their mothers.

Dare to Wear (2015-present). Shed Media/TLC. Social experiment/makeover in which participants swap wardrobes.

Dash Dolls (2015-present). Seacrest Productions/E! Entertainment Television. Reality series set in clothing boutique owned by Kardashians. *Keeping Up with the Kardashians* spin-off.

Deadliest Catch (2005-present). Original Productions/Discovery Channel. Reality series about Alaskan crab fisherman.

Dirty Jobs (2005–12). Pilgrim Films and Television/DCI/Discovery Channel. Reality series about people with unusual or messy occupations.

Divorce Court (1957–69; 1985–92; 1999-present). Kushner/Lock Company/ Monet Lane Productions/20th Century Fox. Reality courtroom show program emphasizing divorce cases.

The Doctors (2008-present). Stage 28 Productions/CBS. Daytime talk show offering medical advice.

Downsized (2010). Pie Town Productions/Women's Entertainment Television (WE). Reality series about a family experiencing unemployment and foreclosure.

Dr. Oz (2009-present). Harpo Productions/Oz Works/Zo Co Productions/ Sony Pictures Television. Daytime health advice program featuring Dr. Mehmet Oz. Spin-off of *The Oprah Winfrey Show*.

Dr. Phil (2002-present). Harpo Productions/King World Productions/Paramount Domestic Television/CBS Television Distribution. Daytime talk show/ self-help program with psychologist and author Phillip McGraw. Spin-off of *The Oprah Winfrey Show*.

Dr. Ruth (1984–91). Lifetime Television. Sex advice program with author, expert and radio personality Ruth Westheimer.

Duck Dynasty (2012-present). Gurney Productions/A&E Television Networks. Reality series about entrepreneurial family in rural Louisiana.

Emeril Live (1997–2010). Food Network/Cooking Channel. Cooking program taped in front of live audience featuring chef Emeril Lagasse.

Everyday Italian (2003-present). Scripps Productions/Teale Edward Productions/ Food Network. Cooking instruction with Giada De Laurentiis.

Extreme Cheapskates (2012-present). Stephen David Entertainment/TLC. Reality series about exceptionally frugal people.

Extreme Cougar Wives (2012). Stiletto Television/TLC. Reality series about women partnered with younger men.

Extreme Couponing (2010–12). Sharp Entertainment/TLC. Reality series about people who actively collect and redeem coupons.

Extreme Makeover (2002–07). Lighthearted Entertainment/New Screen Entertainment/ABC. Makeover program involving plastic surgery.

Extreme Makeover: Home Edition (2003–12). Lock and Key Productions/Endemol Entertainment/ABC. Charity intervention/home makeover.

Fairy Job Mother (2010). Studio Lambert/Lifetime. Makeover focused on the unemployed. Based on U.K. series.

Fix My Life (2012-present). Harpo Studios/Discovery Communications/Oprah Winfrey Network (OWN). Self-help program featuring inspirational speaker Iyanla Vanzant. Also known as *Iyanla, Fix My Life*.

Flip It to Win It (2013-present). Johlt Productions/HGTV. Reality series about entrepreneurs who purchase and rehab foreclosed homes.

Flip or Flop (2013-present). Pie Town Productions/HGTV. Reality series about a family business involving the renovation of foreclosed homes.

Flip This House (2005–09). Departure Films/Trademark Productions/A&E Television Networks. Reality series about buying and renovating homes for profit.

Food Network Star (2005-present). CBS Eye Productions/Triage Entertainment/Food Network. Competition for aspiring TV cooking show hosts. Formerly known as *Next Food Network Star*.

The French Chef (1963–73). WGBH/Public Broadcasting Service (PBS). French cooking instruction with host Julia Child.

From G's to Gents (2008–09). Cris Abrego Productions/Foxxhole Productions/MTV. Competition/makeover program for disadvantaged young men with criminal backgrounds.

Girl Code (2013-present). Viacom Media Networks/MTV. Talk show/advice program for young women with comedic elements.

Glam God with Vivica A. Fox (2008). Cris Abrego Productions/VH1. Competition for aspiring fashion stylists.

Good Eats (1999–2012). Be Square Productions/Mean Street Productions/Food Network/Cooking Channel. Cooking and food commentary with host Alton Brown.

Great Big Benefits Wedding (2015). Channel 5. Reality show in which people on government assistance wed on camera. U.K. series.

Gypsy Sisters (2013–15). Firecracker Films/TLC. Reality series about American women with Roma heritage.

Heavy (2011). Megalomedia/A&E Television Networks. Reality series about subjects of a treatment program for obesity.

Hell's Kitchen (2005-present). Granada Entertainment/Fox Film Network/Fox Television. Cooking competition hosted by celebrity chef Gordon Ramsey. Based on U.K. series.

Here Comes Honey Boo Boo (2012–14). Authentic Entertainment/TLC. Reality sitcom about white, lower-income family in the rural South. Spin-off of *Toddlers and Tiaras*.

HGTV Star (2006–13). 495 Productions/CBS Eye Productions/HGTV. Competition to host home design show. Formerly known as *HGTV Design Star*.

The Hills (2006–10). Done and Done Productions/MTV. Reality series about upscale young women in Los Angeles. Spin off of *Laguna Beach: The Real Orange County*.

Hoarders (2009–13). Screaming Fleas Productions/A&E Television Networks. Reality series documenting and offering assistance to people classified as hoarders.

Hoarders: Family Secrets (2015). Screaming Fleas Productions/Lifetime. Reality series documenting and offering assistance to people classified as hoarders.

Hoarding: Buried Alive (2010–13). Discovery Studios/TLC. Reality series documenting and offering assistance to people classified as hoarders.

Hollywood Unzipped: Stylist Wars (2012). Original Media/Oxygen. Reality series about Hollywood fashion stylists.

Home Made Simple (2011-present). Green Harbor Productions/Oprah Winfrey Network (OWN). Instruction and advice for home organization and simple living.

How Clean Is Your House? (2004–11). Fremantle North American Media/Lifetime. How-to advice instruction/makeover with hosts Aggie MacKenzie and Kim Woodburn. Based on U.K. series.

How to Boil Water (1993-present). Food Network. Cooking instruction.

How to Look Good Naked (2008–10). Maverick Television/RDF Media/Lifetime. Makeover program emphasizing size acceptance and self-esteem. Based on U.K. series.

House Hunters (1999-present). Pie Town Productions/HGTV. Real estate program.

House of DVF (2014-present). Hud:sun Media/E! Entertainment Television. Competition to become the brand ambassador for fashion designer Diane Von Furstenberg.

Houston Beauty (2013). Park Slop Productions/Oprah Winfrey Network (OWN). Reality series set in beauty school.

Human Resources (2014). Left/Right/Pivot TV. Reality show about young people involved in recycling initiatives.

I Am Cait (2015-present). Bunim-Murray Productions/E! Entertainment Television. Reality series about transgender reality TV star Caitlyn Jenner.

I Am Jazz (2015-present). This is Just a Test/TLC. Reality series about a transgender teenager.

Iron Chef America (2005-present). Triage Entertainment/Food Network. Cooking competition. Based on Japanese series.

Jack Lalanne Show (1951–85). BeFit Enterprises. Exercise instruction.

Jamie Oliver's Food Revolution (2010–11). Fresh One Productions/Ryan Seacrest Productions/Channel 4(UK)/ABC. Reality series about a chef's attempt to fight obesity. Known as Jamie's American Food Revolution in U.K.

Jamie's 30 Minute Meals (2010). Fresh One Productions/Channel 4. Cooking instruction with chef Jamie Oliver. U.K. series.

Jerry Springer Show (1991-present). Multimedia Entertainment Inc./NBC Universal Television/Universal Television/Studios USA Television. Daytime talk show with ordinary people as guests.

Jersey Shore (2009–12). 495 Productions/MTV. Reality series about young adults billed as Italian Americans.

Judge Joe Brown (1997–2013). Paramount Domestic Television/Big Ticket Television/CBS Paramount Domestic Television. Reality courtroom program involving disputes among ordinary people.

Judge Judy (1996-present). Paramount Domestic Television/Big Ticket Television/CBS Paramount Domestic Television. Reality courtroom program resolving disputes among ordinary people.

Keeping Up with the Kardashians (2007-present). Bunim-Murray Productions/Ryan Seacrest Productions/E! Entertainment Television. Reality series chronicling Kim, Kourtney and Khloe Kardashian and their family members.

Kourtney and Khloe Take the Hamptons (2014-present). Spin-off of Keeping Up with the Kardashians.

Kourtney and Kim Take Miami (2009–13). Spin-off of Keeping Up with the Kardashians.

Kourtney and Kim Take New York (2011–12). Spin-off of Keeping Up with the Kardashians.

LA Hair (2012-present). 3 Ball Entertainment/Women's Entertainment Television (WE). Reality series about celebrity hair stylist and her salon employees.

Ladette to Lady (2005–10). RDF Media/ITV. Makeover emphasizing feminine manners and etiquette. U.K. series.

Lifestyles of the Rich and Famous (1984–95). Leach Entertainment Features/Television Program Enterprises (TPE)/Paramount Television. Tabloid news program covering the lives of celebrities and elites.

The Little Couple (2009-present). LMNO Productions/TLC. Reality series following a married couple of short stature.

Little People, Big World (2006–15). Gay Rosenthal Productions/TLC. Reality series about family with members of short stature.

Little Women LA (2014-present). Kinetic Content/Lifetime. Reality series about women of short stature.

Little Women NY (2015-present). Kinetic Content/Lifetime. Reality series about women of short stature. Spin off of Little Women LA.

Littlest Groom (2004). LMNO Productions/Fox Television. Dating competition involving people of short stature.

Living with Ed (2007–10). Brentwood Communications International/HGTV/Planet Green. Reality series about actor Ed Bagley, Jr.'s environmentally-conscious lifestyle.

Love and Hip Hop (2010-present). Interloc Films/VH1. Reality series about women involved in the hip hop industry. Also known as *Love and Hip Hop: New York*.

Love and Hip Hop: Atlanta (2012-present). Monami Entertainment/VH1. Reality series about women involved in the hip hop industry.

Love and Hip Hop: Hollywood (2014-present). Monami Entertainment/VH1. Reality series about women involved in the hip hop industry.

Love, Lust or Run (2015-present). ProductionBeast/TLC. Makeover program with former *What Not to Wear* host Stacy London.

Marriage Boot Camp (2013-present). ThinkFactory Media/Women's Entertainment Television (WE). Self-help intervention for couples. Also known as *Marriage Boot Camp: Bridezillas* and *Marriage Boot Camp: Reality Stars*. Spin-off of *Bridezillas*.

Martha Stewart Living (1993–2005). Eyemark Entertainment/Martha Stewart Living Omnimedia/King World Productions. Instruction on cooking, entertaining and housekeeping.

MasterChef (2010-present). One Potato Two Potato/Reveille Productions/Shine Television/Fox Television Network. Cooking competition featuring amateur cooks.

Million Dollar Listing (2006-present). World of Wonder/Bravo. Real estate program following high-end real estate agents in Los Angeles. Also known as *Million Dollar Listing: Los Angeles*.

Million Dollar Listing: Miami (2014-present). World of Wonder/Bravo. Real estate program following high-end real estate agents in Miami.

Million Dollar Listing: New York (2012-present). Real estate program following high-end real estate agents in New York.

Million Dollar Listing: San Francisco (2015-present). Real estate program following high-end real estate agents in San Francisco.

Million Dollar Shopper (2013). True Entertainment/Lifetime. Reality series about personal shoppers.

Millionaire Matchmaker (2008-present). Intuitive Entertainment/Bayonne Entertainment/Bravo. Reality series about matchmaker specializing in wealthy clients.

Mission: Organization (2003–07). Nancy Glass Productions/HGTV. Advice on home organization and de-cluttering.

Molto Mario (1996–2010). Food Network. Cooking instruction with celebrity chef Mario Batali.

More to Love (2009). Warner Horizon Television/Fox Television. Dating competition with plus-sized contestants.

My 600-lb Life (2012-present). Megalomedia/TLC. Reality series about gastric bypass patients.

My Big Fat American Gypsy Wedding (2012-present). Firecracker Films/Discovery Communications/TLC. Reality series about weddings of American couples of Roma heritage.

My Big Fat Fabulous Life (2015-present). Pilgrim Studios/TLC. Reality series about YouTube star who refuses to be stigmatized as overweight.

My Five Wives (2013–14). Relativity Television/Bogner Productions/TLC. Reality series about polygamous family.

My Shopping Addiction (2012–13). Screaming Flea Productions/Oxygen. Reality series about people addicted to shopping.

My Strange Addiction (2010-present). Reality series about people with unusual or compulsive behaviors. Violet Media/20 West Productions/TLC.

Mystery Diagnosis (2005–11). True Entertainment/Discovery Health/Oprah Winfrey Network (OWN). Reality series profiling mysterious and difficult medical cases.

Nail'd It (2014). Matador/Oxygen. Competition among manicurists/nail designers.

Nail Files (2011–13). 495 Productions/TV Guide Network. Reality series about the owner of an upscale nail salon with a celebrity clientele.

Naked Chef (1999–2001). Optomen Television/BBC2/Food Network. U.K. series with U.S. distribution.

Nigella Bites (2000–07). Flashback Television/Channel 4/Food Network. Cooking instruction with Nigella Lawson. U.K. series with U.S. distribution.

Nigella Kitchen (2010). BBC2/Food Network. Cooking instruction with Nigella Lawson. U.K. series with U.S. distribution.

One Big Happy Family (2010). Zodiak USA/TLC. Reality series about family struggling to lose weight.

Oprah Winfrey Show (1986–2011). Harpo Productions/High Noon Productions/ King World Productions/CBS Paramount International Television. Daytime talk show with host Oprah Winfrey.

Parents Just Don't Understand (2014). 51 Minds Entertainment/Hub. Reality series in which teens and parents swap lives.

Pioneer Woman (2011-present). Pacific/Food Network. Cooking and lifestyle advice with host Ree Drummond.

Project Runway (2004-present). Bunim-Murray Productions/Bravo/Lifetime. Competition among aspiring fashion designers.

Property Brothers (2011-present). Cineflix/W Network/HGTV. Canadian real estate program with U.S. distribution.

Push Girls (2012–13). Gay Rosenthal Productions/Sundance. Reality series about a group of women who are paralyzed.

Queer Eye for the Straight Guy (2003–07). Scout Productions/Bravo Original Productions/Bravo. Makeover in which gay stylists offer advice to heterosexual men.

Rachel Zoe Project (2008–13). Original Media/Hunting Lane Films/Bravo. Reality series about celebrity stylist Rachel Zoe.

Real Housewives of Atlanta (2008-present). True Entertainment/Bravo. Docusoap about upscale female friend group.

Real Housewives of Beverly Hills (2010-present). Evolution Media/Bravo. Docusoap about upscale female friend group.

Real Housewives of Miami (2011–13). MC Filmworks/Purveyors of Pop/Bravo. Docusoap about upscale female friend group.

Real Housewives of New Jersey (2009-present). Sirens Media/Bravo. Docusoap about upscale female friend group.

Real Housewives of New York (2008-present). Ricochet Television/Bravo. Docusoap about upscale female friend group.

Real Housewives of Orange County (2006-present). Dunlop Entertainment/Evolution Film and Tape/Kaufman Films/Bravo. Docusoap about upscale female friend group. First in the *Real Housewives* franchise.

The Real World (1992-present). Bunim-Murray Productions/MTV. Reality series/social experiment with revolving locations and casts of young people.

Return to Amish (2014). Hot Snakes Media/TLC. Reality series about rebellious young people returning to Amish communities. Spin-off of *Breaking Amish*.

Rich Kids of Beverly Hills (2014-present). ITV Studios America/Leepson Bounds Entertainment/E! Entertainment Television. Reality series about wealthy friend group.

RuPaul's Drag Race (2009-present). Wonder of Wonder/Logo Television Network. Competition to become the next drag superstar.

RuPaul's Drag Race Untucked (2010-present). Wonder of Wonder/Logo Television Network. Behind-the-scenes at *RuPaul's Drag Race*.

The Salon (2003–04). Endemol UK/Channel 4. Reality series set in working beauty salon manufactured for television. U.K. series.

Shahs of Sunset (2012-present). Ryan Seacrest Productions/Bravo. Reality series about affluent Persian friends.

Shear Genius (2007–10). Reveille Productions/Bravo. Competition among professional hairstylists.

Sister Wives (2010-present). Puddle Monkey Productions/Figure 8 Films/TLC. Reality series about polygamous family.

Style by Jury (2015-present). Electus Productions/TLC. Fashion makeover. Based on global format.

Styl'd (2009). Bunim-Murray Productions/MTV. Reality series about up-and-coming fashion stylists.

Styled by June (2012). Ish Entertainment/VH1. Reality series chronicling celebrity fashion stylist June Ambrose.

Sunset Tan (2007–08). Intuitive Entertainment/E! Entertainment Television. Reality series set in tanning salon.

Supernanny (2005–12). Ricochet Television/Shed Media/ABC. Intervention/parenting advice program. Based on U.K. series.

Survivor (2000-present). Mark Burnett Productions/Castaway Productions/CBS. Survivalist gamedoc set in remote locations. Based on global format.

The Suze Orman Show (2002–15). CNBC. Financial advice.

Swamp People (2010-present). Original Media/History Channel. Reality series about alligator hunters in rural Louisiana.

Tabatha's Salon Takeover (2008–13). Reveille Productions/Take It Over Productions/Bravo. Makeover program focused on hair salon owners and employees.

Teen Mom (2009-present). 11th Street Productions/MTV. Reality series following four teenage mothers. Spin-off of *16 and Pregnant*.

Teen Mom 2 (2011-present). Spin off of *Teen Mom* with new cast members.

Teen Mom 3 (2013). Spin off of *Teen Mom* with new cast members.

T. I.'s Road to Redemption (2009). Ish Entertainment/MTV. Intervention by rap star to deter criminal behavior.

Tiny House, Big Living (2014-present). Orion Entertainment/HGTV. Interior design advice for tiny house owners.

Tiny House Builders (2014-present). Pie Town Productions/HGTV. Reality series following tiny house designer.

Tiny House Hunters (2014-present). Pie Town Productions/HGTV. Reality series about people downsizing to tiny houses.

Tiny House Nation (2014-present). Loud Television/FYI. Reality series about designers and builders of tiny houses.

Toddlers and Tiaras (2009–13). Authentic Entertainment/Discovery Communications/TLC. Reality series about child beauty pageant contestants and their families.

Top Chef (2006-present). Magical Elves Productions/Bravo. Competition among chefs.

Top Design (2007–08). Stone and Company Entertainment/Bravo. Contest for aspiring interior designers.

Tough Love (2009–13). Flower Films/High Noon Entertainment/VH1. Matchmaking/makeover program for unmarried women.

Trailer Park: Welcome to Myrtle Manor (2013-present). Jupiter Entertainment/TLC. Reality series about the residents of a South Carolina trailer park. Also known as Myrtle Manor.

True Beauty (2009). Bankable Productions/Katalyst Films/Warner Horizon Television/ABC. Beauty contest emphasizing inner beauty.

True Life (1998-present). Bandito Films/Gigantic! Productions/Moxie Firecracker Films/Shadowbox Films/MTV. Documentary series about unusual identities and experiences.

Wa$ted (2007). Lion Television/Discovery Communications/Planet Green. Eco-themed intervention/makeover.

What Not to Wear (2003–13). BBC Production USA/Discovery Communications/TLC. Makeover program. Based on U.K. series.

Wife Swap (2004–10). RFD Media/ABC/Lifetime. Social experiment in which wives trade places. Based on global format.

Work of Art: The Next Great Artist (2010–2011). Magical Elves Productions/Pretty Matches Productions/Bravo. Competition among aspiring artists.

Work Out (2006–08). Mentorn USA/Bravo. Reality series about fitness trainers with elite clienteles.

INDEX

class: blurring distinctions 55; and casting 130; commodification of 22, 128; and creative labor 111–12, 117; and homemaking 103–4; inequalities 19, 30, 48, 52, 59, 82, 137, 143; as lifestyle choice 55–6, 58, 84; and makeovers 55, 80, 85, 142; and marketing 30–1, 38; and othering 131, 133, 136; as performance 84, 126, 136–7, 147; representation of 8, 9, 16–17, 19–20, 59–60, 65, 84, 113–14, 131, 133–4, 137–8; and sexual reproduction 92–3, 95; *see also* middle class, working class
cleaning 102, 105
clutter 104–5
Cohen, Lizbeth 29–30
comedy 8, 10, 65–6, 125, 132–3, 138, 142
commodification 27, 43, 121–2
commodity fetishism 100
competition 6, 13, 57, 69, 71, 84, 85, 122, 146; *see also* talent competition
conduct 11, 60–2, 76–79; *see also* governmentality
confessional 128, 132, 146
consumption 29, 36, 54, 56, 141, 145; and authenticity 58; and citizenship 85–8, 139; and expertise 32, 59, 63–4; and identity 1, 57–9, 146; and race 135, 141, 143; as reflexive 54–6, 58–9
cooking 11–12, 32–4, 52, 64, 71, 100–4, 121, 150
Cooking Channel 32
Corner, John 74, 126, 134, 136
corporate social responsibility (CSR) 75, 84, 90
Couldry, Nick 145–46
crafts 34

creative industries 101, 111–12, 117, 119
creative labor 101, 119, 122
crime 82–3, 130
cultural capital 137–8; *see also* taste
cultural intermediaries *see* intermediaries
Cupcake Wars (series) 34, 71
Curb Appeal (series) 71
Curtin, Michael 29

Dad Camp (series) 90
Dance Moms (series) 2
dandy 55, 58, 85
Dash Dolls (series) 44
dating 5, 16, 57, 66, 70, 89, 131, 147
daytime television 15–16, 80, 86, 106
Deadliest Catch (series) 113
debt 59
democracy 74, 76, 78, 150
demographics 31, 130
deregulation 29, 74, 69, 100, 129
diet 71, 76, 88, 89; *see also* nutrition
difference: commodification of 4, 21, 126–7, 130, 142, 148; as consumer identity 4, 14, 16, 133; and othering 9, 19, 126, 131–4; 138; performance of 22, 128, 136–7, 139–40, 147; politics of 10, 127; proliferation of 4, 9, 145
digital media 26, 29, 36, 39, 42, 61, 95, 118; *see also* class, disability, ethnicity, race
Dirty Jobs (series) 113
disability 130–31
Discovery Communications 35, 42, 58, 125
Discovery Health 96, 150
diversity 19, 142, 144
Divorce Court (series) 16
DIY Network 32